Sonnets and Verse

Sonnets and Verse

by

H. Belloc

Duckworth

3 Henrietta Street, London, W.C.

First Published October 1923
New Edition, with many new Poems, May 1938
Reprinted, July 1938; January 1940; September 1941;
August 1944 and May 1945

MADE AND PRINTED IN GREAT BRITAIN BY
MORRISON AND GIBB LTD., LONDON AND EDINBURGH

CONTENTS

I. SONNETS

CONTENTS

CONTENTS

II. LYRICAL, DIDACTIC AND GROTESQUE

CONTENTS

III. SONGS

CONTENTS

IV. BALLADES

CONTENTS

I
SONNETS

SONNETS

I

Lift up your hearts in Gumber, laugh the Weald
And you my mother the Valley of Arun sing.
Here am I homeward from my wandering,
Here am I homeward and my heart is healed.
You my companions whom the World has tired
Come out to greet me.   I have found a face
More beautiful than Gardens ; more desired
Than boys in exile love their native place.

Lift up your hearts in Gumber, laugh the Weald
And you most ancient Valley of Arun sing.
Here am I homeward from my wandering,
Here am I homeward and my heart is healed.
If I was thirsty, I have heard a spring.
If I was dusty, I have found a field.

3

SONNETS

II

I was like one that keeps the deck by night
   Bearing the tiller up against his breast;
I was like one whose soul is centred quite
   In holding course although so hardly prest,
And veers with veering shock now left now right,
   And strains his foothold still and still makes play
Of bending beams until the sacred light
   Shows him high lands and heralds up the day.

But now such busy work of battle past
I am like one whose barque at bar at last
Comes hardly heeling down the adventurous breeze;
And entering calmer seas,
I am like one that brings his merchandise
To Californian skies.

III

Rise up and do begin the day's adorning;
The Summer dark is but the dawn of day.
The last of sunset fades into the morning;
The morning calls you from the dark away.
The holy mist, the white mist of the morning
Was wreathing upward on my lonely way.
The way was waiting for your own adorning
That should complete the broad adornéd day.

Rise up and do begin the day's adorning;
The little eastern clouds are dapple grey:
There will be wind among the leaves to-day;
It is the very promise of the morning.
  Lux Tua Via Mea: your light's my way—
Then do rise up and make it perfect day.

IV

THE Winter Moon has such a quiet car
That all the winter nights are dumb with rest.
She drives the gradual dark with drooping crest
And dreams go wandering from her drowsy star
Because the nights are silent do not wake
But there shall tremble through the general earth,
And over you, a quickening and a birth.
The Sun is near the hill-tops for your sake.

The latest born of all the days shall creep
To kiss the tender eyelids of the year;
And you shall wake, grown young with perfect
    sleep,
And smile at the new world and make it dear
  With living murmurs more than dreams are deep;
  Silence is dead, my dawn, the morning's here.

SONNETS

V

WHATEVER moisture nourishes the Rose,
The Rose of the World in laughter's garden-bed
Where Souls of men on faith secure are fed
And spirits immortal keep their pleasure-close.
Whatever moisture nourishes the Rose,
The burning Rose of the world, for me the same
To-day for me the spring without a name
Content or Grace or Laughter overflows.

This is that water from the Fount of Gold
Water of Youth and washer out of cares
Which Raymond of Saragossa sought of old
And finding in the mountain, unawares,
Returned to hear an ancient story told
To Bramimond, his love, beside the marble stairs.

SONNETS

VI

YOUTH gave you to me, but I'll not believe
That Youth will, taking his quick self, take you.
Youth's all our Truth: he cannot so deceive.
He has our graces, not our ownselves too.
He still compares with time when he'll be spent,
By human doom enhancing what we are;
Enriches us with rare experiment,
Lends arms to leagured Age in Time's rough war.

Look! This Youth in us is an Old Man taking
A Boy to make him wiser than his days.
So is our old Youth our young Age's making:
So rich in time our final debt he pays.
　　Then with your quite young arms do you me hold
　　And I will still be young when all the World's
　　　　grown old.

SONNETS

VII

MORTALITY is but the Stuff you wear
To show the better on the imperfect sight.
Your home is surely with the changeless light
Of which you are the daughter and the heir.
For as you pass, the natural life of things
Proclaims the Resurrection : as you pass
Remembered summer shines across the grass
And somewhat in me of the immortal sings.

You were not made for memory, you are not
Youth's accident I think but heavenly more ;
Moulding to meaning slips my pen's poor blot
And opening wide that long forbidden door
 Where stands the Mother of God, your exemplar.
 How beautiful, how beautiful you are !

VIII

NOT for the luckless buds our roots may bear
  Now all in bloom, now seared and cankered lying
Will I entreat you, lest they should compare
  Foredoomed humanity with the fall of flowers.
Hold thou with me the chaste communion rare
  And touch with life this mortal case of ours:
  You're lifted up beyond the power of dying:
I die, as bounded things die everywhere.

  You're voiced companionship, I'm silence lonely;
You're stuff, I'm void; you're living, I'm decay.
  I fall, I think, to-night and ending only;
You rise, I know, through still advancing day.
  And knowing living gift were life for me
  In narrow room of rhyme I fixed it certainly.

10

SONNETS

IX

THAT which is one they shear and make it twain
Who would Love's light and dark discriminate:
His pleasure is one essence with his pain,
Even his desire twin brother to his hate.
With him the foiled attempt is half achieving;
And being mastered, to be armed a lord;
And doubting every chance is still believing;
And losing all one's own is all reward.

I am acquainted with misfortune's fortune,
And better than herself her dowry know:
For she that is my fortune and misfortune,
Making me hapless, makes me happier so:
In which conceit, as older men may prove,
Lies manifest the verv core of Love.

11

SONNETS

X

SHALL any man for whose strong love another
   Has thrown away his wealth and name in one,
Shall he turn mocker of a more than brother
   To slight his need when his adventure's done ?
Or shall a breedless boy whose mother won him
   In great men's great concerns his little place
Turn when his farthing honours come upon him
   To mock her yeoman air and conscious grace ?

Then mock me as you do my narrow scope,
   For you it was put out this light of mine :
Wrongfully wrecked my new adventured hope,
   Wasted my wordy wealth, spilt my rich wine,
Made my square ship within a league of shore
   Alas !   To be entombed in seas and seen no more.

12

SONNETS

THEY that have taken wages of things done
When sense abused has blocked the doors of sense.
They that have lost their heritage of the sun,
Their laughter and their holy innocence ;
They turn them now to this thing, now to t'other,
For anchor hold against swift-eddying time,
Some to that square of earth which was their mother,
And some to noisy fame, and some to rhyme.

But I to that far morning where you stood
In fullness of the body, with your hands
Reposing on your walls, before your lands,
And all, together, making one great good :
   Then did I cry " For this my birth was meant.
   These are my use, and this my sacrament ! "

XII

BEAUTY that Parent is to deathless Rhyme
Was Manhood's maker: you shall bear a Son,
Till Daughters linked adown admiring time
Fulfil the mother, handing Beauty on.
You shall by breeding make Life answer yet,
In Time's despite, Time's jeer that men go void;
Your stamp of heaven shall be more largely set
Than my one joy, ten thousand times enjoyed.

The glories of our state and its achievement,
Which wait their passing, shall not pass away.
I will extend our term beyond bereavement,
And launch our date into a dateless day.
    For you shall make recórd, and when that's sealed
    In Beauty made immortal, all is healed.

XIII

WHAT are the names for Beauty ? Who shall praise
God's pledge he can fulfil His creatures' eyes ?
Or what strong words of what creative phrase
Determine Beauty's title in the skies ?
But I will call you Beauty Personate,
Ambassadorial Beauty, and again
Beauty triumphant, Beauty in the Gate,
Beauty salvation of the souls of men.

For Beauty was not Beauty till you came
And now shall Beauty mean the sign you are;
A Beacon burnt above the Dawn, a flame
Like holy Lucifer the Morning Star,
 Who latest hangs in Heaven and is the gem
 On all the widowéd Night's expectant Diadem.

XIV

LOVE wooing Honour, Honour's love did win
And had his pleasure all a summer's day
Not understanding how the dooms begin,
Love wooing Honour, wooed her life away.
Then wandered he a full five years unrest
Until, one night, this Honour that had died
Came as he slept, in youth grown glorified
And smiling like the Saints whom God has blest.

But when he saw her on the clear night shine
Serene with more than mortal light upon her,
The boy that careless was of things divine,
Small Love, turned penitent to worship Honour.
    So Love can conquer Honour : when that's past
    Dead Honour risen outdoes Love at last.

XV

YOUR life is like a little winter's day
Whose sad sun rises late to set too soon;
You have just come—why will you go away,
Making an evening of what should be noon.
Your life is like a little flute complaining
A long way off, beyond the willow trees:
A long way off, and nothing left remaining
But memory of a music on the breeze.

Your life is like a pitiful leave-taking
Wept in a dream before a man's awaking,
A Call with only shadows to attend:
A Benediction whispered and belated
Which has no fruit beyond a consecrated,
A consecrated silence at the end.

XVI

Now shall the certain purpose of my soul
By blind and empty things controlled be,
And mine audacious course to that far goal
Fall short, confessing mere mortality.
Limbs shall have movement and ignore their living,
Brain wit, that he his quickness may deny.
My promised hope forswears in act of giving,
Time eats me up and makes my words a lie.

And mine unbounded dream has found a bar,
And I must worst deceit of best things bear.
Now dawn's but daybreak, seas but waters are,
Night darkness only, all wide heaven just air:
　　And you to whom these fourteen lines I tell,
　　My beauty, my desire : but not my love as well

XVII

BECAUSE my faltering feet may fail to dare
The first descendant of the steps of Hell
Give me the Word in time that triumphs there.
I too must pass into the misty hollow
Where all our living laughter stops : and hark !
The tiny stuffless voices of the dark
Have called me, called me, till I needs must follow :
Give me the Word and I'll attempt it well.

Say it's the little winking of an eye
Which in that issue is uncurtained quite ;
A little sleep that helps a moment by
Between the thin dawn and the large daylight.
   Ah ! tell me more than yet was hoped of men ;
   Swear that's true now, and I'll believe it then.

XVIII

Whᴇɴ you to Acheron's ugly water come
Where darkness is and formless mourners brood
And down the shelves of that distasteful flood
Survey the human rank in order dumb.
When the pale dead go forward, tortured more
By nothingness and longing than by fire,
Which bear their hands in suppliance with desire,
With stretched desire for the ulterior shore.

Then go before them like a royal ghost
And tread like Egypt or like Carthage crowned;
Because in your Mortality the most
Of all we may inherit has been found—
  Children for memory: the Faith for pride.
  Good land to leave: and young Love satisfied.

SONNETS

XIX

WE will not whisper, we have found the place
Of silence and the endless halls of sleep.
And that which breathes alone throughout the deep
The end and the beginning : and the face
Between the level brows of whose blind eyes
Lie plenary contentment, full surcease
Of violence, and the passionless long peace
Wherein we lose our human lullabies.

Look up and tell the immeasurable height
Between the vault of the world and your dear head ;
That's death, my little sister, and the night
Which was our Mother beckons us to bed,
   Where large oblivion in her house is laid
    For us tired children, now our games are played.

SONNETS

XX

I WENT to sleep at Dawn in Tuscany
Beneath a Rock and dreamt a morning dream.
I thought I stood by that baptismal stream
Whereon the bounds of our redemption lie.
And there, beyond, a radiance rose to take
My soul at passing, in which light your eyes
So filled me I was drunk with Paradise.
Then the day broadened, but I did not wake.

Here's the last edge of my long parchment furled
And all was writ that you might read it so.
This sleep I swear shall last the length of day;
Not noise, not chance, shall drive this dream away:
Not time, not treachery, not good fortune—no,
Not all the weight of all the wears of the world.

XXI

Almighty God, whose justice like a sun
Shall coruscate along the floors of Heaven,
Raising what's low, perfecting what's undone,
Breaking the proud and making odd things even.
The poor of Jesus Christ along the street
In your rain sodden, in your snows unshod,
They have nor hearth, nor sword, nor human meat,
Nor even the bread of men : Almighty God.

The poor of Jesus Christ whom no man hears
Have waited on your vengeance much too long.
Wipe out not tears but blood : our eyes bleed tears.
Come smite our damnéd sophistries so strong
That thy rude hammer battering this rude wrong
Ring down the abyss of twice ten thousand years.

SONNETS

XXII

MOTHER of all my cities once there lay
  About your weedy wharves an orient shower
  Of spice and languorous silk and all the dower
That Ocean gave you on his bridal day.
And now the youth and age have passed away
  And all the sail superb and all the power;
  Your time's a time of memory like that hour
Just after sunset, wonderful and grey.

Too tired to rise and much too sad to weep,
  With strong arm nerveless on a nerveless knee,
Still to your slumbering ears the spousal deep
  Murmurs his thoughts of eld eternally;
But your soul wakes not from its holy sleep
Dreaming of dead delights beside a tideless sea.

SONNETS

XXIII

November is that historied Emperor
   Conquered in age but foot to foot with fate
Who from his refuge high has heard the roar
   Of squadrons in pursuit, and now, too late,
Stirrups the storm and calls the winds to war,
   And arms the garrison of his last heirloom,
And shakes the sky to its extremest shore
   With battle against irrevocable doom.

Till, driven and hurled from his strong citadels,
   He flies in hurrying cloud and spurs him on,
Empty of lingerings, empty of farewells
   And final benedictions and is gone.
But in my garden all the trees have shed
Their legacies of the light and all the flowers are dead.

SONNETS

XXIV

HOAR Time about the House betakes him slow
Seeking an entry for his weariness.
And in that dreadful company distress
And the sad night with silent footsteps go.
On my poor fire the brands are scarce aglow
And in the woods without what memories press
Where, waning in the trees from less to less
Mysterious hangs the hornéd moon and low.

For now December, full of agéd care
Comes in upon the year and weakly grieves;
Mumbling his lost desires and his despair
And with mad trembling hand still interweaves
The dank sear flower-stalks tangled in his hair,
While round about him whirl the rotten leaves.

SONNETS

XXV

IT freezes : all across a soundless sky
The birds go home.   The governing dark's begun.
The steadfast dark that waits not for a sun ;
The ultimate dark wherein the race shall die.
Death with his evil finger to his lip
Leers in at human windows, turning spy
To learn the country where his rule shall lie
When he assumes perpetual generalship.

The undefeated enemy, the chill
That shall benumb the voiceful earth at last,
Is master of our moment, and has bound
The viewless wind itself.   There is no sound.
It freezes.   Every friendly stream is fast.
It freezes, and the graven twigs are still.

XXVI

O MY companion, O my sister Sleep,
The valley is all before us, bear me on.
High through the heaven of evening, hardly gone,
Beyond the harbour lights, beyond the steep,
Beyond the land and its lost benison
To where, majestic on the darkening deep,
The night comes forward from Mount Aurion.
O my companion, O my sister Sleep.

Above the surf-line, into the night-breeze;
Eastward above the ever-whispering seas;
Through the warm airs with no more watch to keep.
My day's run out and all its dooms are graven.
O dear forerunner of Death and promise of Haven.
O my companion, O my sister Sleep.

SONNETS

XXVII

ARE you the end, Despair, or the poor least
   Of them that cast great shadows and are lies ?
   That dread the simple and destroy the wise,
Fail at the tomb and triumph at the feast ?
You were not found on Olivet, dull beast,
   Nor in Thebaid, when the night's agonies
   Dissolved to glory on the effulgent east
And Jesus Christ was in the morning skies.

You did not curb the indomitable crest
   Of Tzerna-Gora, when the Falcon-bred
     Screamed over the Adriatic, and their Lord
Went riding out, much angrier than the rest,
   To summon at ban the living and the dead
     And break the Mahommedan with the repeated
     sword.

SONNETS

XXVIII

BUT oh ! not Lovely Helen, nor the pride
Of that most ancient Ilium matched with doom.
Men murdered Priam in his royal room
And Troy was burned with fire and Hector died.
For even Hector's dreadful day was more
Than all his breathing courage dared defend
The armouréd light and bulwark of the war
Trailed his great story to the accustomed end.

He was the city's buttress, Priam's Son,
The Soldier born in bivouac praises great
And horns in double front of battle won.
Yet down he went : when unremembering fate
Felled him at last with all his armour on.
Hector : the horseman : in the Scæan Gate.

SONNETS

XXIX

THE world's a stage.   The light is in one's eyes.
The Auditorium is extremely dark.
The more dishonest get the larger rise ;
The more offensive make the greater mark.
The women on it prosper by their shape,
Some few by their vivacity.   The men,
By tailoring in breeches and in cape.
The world's a stage—I say it once again.

The scenery is very much the best
Of what the wretched drama has to show,
Also the prompter happens to be dumb.
We drink behind the scenes and pass a jest
On all our folly ; then, before we go
Loud cries for " Author " . . . but he doesn't come.

SONNETS

THE world's a stage—and I'm the Super man,
And no one seems responsible for salary.
I roar my part as loudly as I can
And all I mouth I mouth it to the gallery.
I haven't got another rhyme in " alery "
It would have made a better job, no doubt
If I had left attempt at Rhyming out,
Like Alfred Tennyson adapting Malory.

The world's a stage, the company of which
Has very little talent and less reading :
But many a waddling heathen painted bitch
And many a standing cad of gutter breeding.
    We sweat to learn our book : for all our pains
    We pass.   The Chucker-out alone remains.

SONNETS

XXXI

THE world's a stage.   The trifling entrance fee
Is paid (by proxy) to the registrar.
The Orchestra is very loud and free
But plays no music in particular.
They do not print a programme, that I know.
The caste is large.   There isn't any plot.
The acting of the piece is far below
The very worst of modernistic rot.

The only part about it I enjoy
Is what was called in English the Foyay.
There will I stand apart awhile and toy
With thought, and set my cigarette alight;
And then—without returning to the play—
On with my coat and out into the night.

SONNETS

XXXII

THEY that have been beside us all the day
  Rise up; for they are summoned to the gate.
Nor turn the head but take a downward way;
  Depart, and leave their households desolate.
But you shall not depart, although you leave
  My house for conversation with your peers.
Your admirable Ghost shall not receive
  Mere recollected vows and secret tears.

  But on that brink of Heaven where lingering
      stand
    The still-remembrant spirits hearkening down,
  Go, tower among them all, to hear the land,
    To hear the land alive with your renown.
        Nor strength, nor peace, nor laughter could
          I give
        But this great wages: after death, to live.

34

SONNETS

OF meadows drowsy with Trinacrian bees,
Of shapes that moved a rising mist among—
Persephone between the Cypress trees—
Of lengthier shades along the woodland flung,
Of calm upon the hardly whispering seas,
Of cloud that to the distant island clung—
He made of emerald evening and of these
A holier song than ever yet was sung.

But silence and the single-thoughted night,
Hearing such music took him for their own
To that long land, where, men forgotten quite
Harpless he errs by Lethe stream alone.
He never more will know that wind-flower's white—
He never more shall hear uneasy autumn moan.

XXXIV

Would that I had £300,000
   Invested in some strong security;
A Midland Country House with formal grounds,
   A Town House, and a House beside the sea,
And one in Spain, and one in Normandy,
   And Friends innumerable at my call
And youth serene—and underneath it all
   One steadfast, passionate flame to nurture me.

Then would I chuck for good my stinking trade
   Of writing tosh at 1s. 6d. a quire !
And soar like young Bellerophon arrayed
   High to the filmy Heavens of my desire. . . .
      But that's all over.   Here's the world again.
      Bring me the Blotter.   Fill the fountain-pen.

SONNETS

XXXV

Do not believe when lovely lips report
That I lost anchor in rough seas of jest,
Or turned in false confusion manifest,
To pleading folly in high beauty's court;
Or said of that you do (which in the doing
You maim yourself) what things I could not say,
For dread of unassuaged remorse ensuing
On one light word which haunts us all our way.

That I grow sour, who only lack delight;
That I descend to sneer, who only grieve:
That from my depth I should contemn your height;
That with my blame my mockery you receive;
Huntress and splendour of the woodland night
Diana of this world, do not believe.

XXXVI

BELIEVING Truth is staring at the sun
Which but destroys the power that could perceive.
So naught of our poor selves can be at one
With burning Truth, nor utterly believe.
For we that mortal are, to our derision,
Must soften certitude with that which seems,
And slake in dull repose a blinding vision,
Buy light with dark, and sleep for sake of dreams.

Mistrust, I do require you, all you trust,
And mock continuance of a steadfast mood,
And taste in all your joys their coming dust,
And call the endless flight of goodness, good.
Save in one article—Doubt earth and sea,
Doubt all that stands and is, but doubt not me.

XXXVII

Believe too little and go down despairing;
Believe too much and lose it at the end.
Believe in none and die of over-caring;
Believe in all and die without a friend.
Believe in what's to come and still go grieving;
Believe in what's gone by and find it fades.
Believe in not insisting on believing
For all believing's but a dance of shades.

But oh! believe in me! I ask no more—
And you no more of sustenance shall need;
For that's a food ambrosial which can feed
The soul with sendings from th'Elysian shore,
As though contents eternal breathed abroad.
But don't believe in Phémé; she's a fraud.

XXXVIII

BECAUSE I find foreknowledge in my soul
Of your true sisterhood with heavenly things,
And see from tardier years that further goal
Youth hides from you with its imaginings,
And witness am to your inheritance
And see beneath the passing of your grace
Un-passing calms, and a perfected face
Immutable; prefigured in a glance—

Therefore did I and therefore now complain
That you're profaned, and daily do renew
To make your own resplendent beauty vain
Through mimic beauty of what's likest you.
This was my sentence.   This was all my say;
Mourning such light beclouded in a play.

II

LYRICAL, DIDACTIC AND GROTESQUE

D

TO DIVES

Dives, when you and I go down to Hell,
Where scribblers end and millionaires as well,
We shall be carrying on our separate backs
Two very large but very different packs ;
And as you stagger under yours, my friend,
Down the dull shore where all our journeys end,
And go before me (as your rank demands)
Towards the infinite flat underlands,
And that dear river of forgetfulness—
Charon, a man of exquisite address
(For, as your wife's progenitors could tell,
They're very strict on etiquette in Hell),
Will, since you are a lord, observe, " My lord,
We cannot take these weighty things aboard ! "
Then down they go, my wretched Dives, down—
The fifteen sorts of boots you kept for town ;
The hat to meet the Devil in ; the plain
But costly ties ; the cases of champagne ;
The solid watch, and seal, and chain, and charm ;
The working model of a Burning Farm
(To give the little Belials) ; all the three
Biscuits for Cerberus ; the guarantee
From Lambeth that the Rich can never burn,

And even promising a safe return;
The admirable overcoat, designed
To cross Cocytus—very warmly lined:
Sweet Dives, you will leave them all behind
And enter Hell as tattered and as bare
As was your father when he took the air
Behind a barrow-load in Leicester Square.
Then turned to me, and noting one that brings
With careless step a mist of shadowy things:
Laughter and memories, and a few regrets,
Some honour, and a quantity of debts,
A doubt or two of sorts, a trust in God,
And (what will seem to you extremely odd)
His father's granfer's father's father's name,
Unspoilt, untitled, even spelt the same;
Charon, who twenty thousand times before
Has ferried Poets to the ulterior shore,
Will estimate the weight I bear, and cry—
" Comrade ! "   (He has himself been known
  to try
His hand at Latin and Italian verse,
Much in the style of Virgil—only worse)
" We let such vain imaginaries pass ! "
Then tell me, Dives, which will look the ass—
You, or myself ?   Or Charon ?   Who can tell ?
They order things so damnably in Hell.

STANZAS WRITTEN ON BATTERSEA BRIDGE
DURING A SOUTH-WESTERLY GALE

THE woods and downs have caught the mid-December,
  The noisy woods and high sea-downs of home;
The wind has found me and I do remember
  The strong scent of the foam.

Woods, darlings of my wandering feet, another
  Possesses you, another treads the Down;
The South West Wind that was my elder brother
  Has come to me in town.

The wind is shouting from the hills of morning,
  I do remember and I will not stay.
I'll take the Hampton road without a warning
  And get me clean away.

The channel is up, the little seas are leaping,
  The tide is making over Arun Bar;
And there's my boat, where all the rest are sleeping
  And my companions are.

I'll board her, and apparel her, and I'll mount her,
  My boat, that was the strongest friend to me—

45

ON BATTERSEA BRIDGE

That brought my boyhood to its first encounter
  And taught me the wide sea.

Now shall I drive her, roaring hard a' weather,
  Right for the salt and leave them all behind;
We'll quite forget the treacherous streets together
  And find—or shall we find?

There is no Pilotry my soul relies on
  Whereby to catch beneath my bended hand,
Faint and beloved along the extreme horizon
  That unforgotten land.

We shall not round the granite piers and paven
  To lie to wharves we know with canvas furled.
My little Boat, we shall not make the haven—
  It is not of the world.

Somewhere of English forelands grandly guarded
  It stands, but not for exiles, marked and clean;
Oh! not for us.   A mist has risen and marred it :—
  My youth lies in between.

So in this snare that holds me and appals me,
  Where honour hardly lives nor loves remain,
The Sea compels me and my County calls me,
  But stronger things restrain.

     ·   ·   ·   ·   ·

ON BATTERSEA BRIDGE

England, to me that never have malingered,
   Nor spoken falsely, nor your flattery used,
Nor even in my rightful garden lingered :—
   What have you not refused ?

THE SOUTH COUNTRY

WHEN I am living in the Midlands
  That are sodden and unkind,
I light my lamp in the evening:
  My work is left behind;
And the great hills of the South Country
  Come back into my mind.

The great hills of the South Country
  They stand along the sea;
And it's there walking in the high woods
  That I could wish to be,
And the men that were boys when I was a boy
  Walking along with me.

The men that live in North England
  I saw them for a day:
Their hearts are set upon the waste fells,
  Their skies are fast and grey;
From their castle-walls a man may see
  The mountains far away.

The men that live in West England
  They see the Severn strong,

THE SOUTH COUNTRY

A-rolling on rough water brown
  Light aspen leaves along.
They have the secret of the Rocks,
  And the oldest kind of song.

But the men that live in the South Country
  Are the kindest and most wise,
They get their laughter from the loud surf,
  And the faith in their happy eyes
Comes surely from our Sister the Spring
  When over the sea she flies;
The violets suddenly bloom at her feet,
  She blesses us with surprise.

I never get between the pines
  But I smell the Sussex air;
Nor I never come on a belt of sand
  But my home is there.
And along the sky the line of the Downs
  So noble and so bare.

A lost thing could I never find,
  Nor a broken thing mend:
And I fear I shall be all alone
  When I get towards the end.
Who will there be to comfort me
  Or who will be my friend?

I will gather and carefully make my friends
  Of the men of the Sussex Weald,

THE SOUTH COUNTRY

They watch the stars from silent folds,
   They stiffly plough the field.
By them and the God of the South Country
   My poor soul shall be healed.

If I ever become a rich man,
   Or if ever I grow to be old,
I will build a house with deep thatch
   To shelter me from the cold,
And there shall the Sussex songs be sung
   And the story of Sussex told.

I will hold my house in the high wood
   Within a walk of the sea,
And the men that were boys when I was a boy
   Shall sit and drink with me.

THE FANATIC

Last night in Compton Street, Soho,
A man whom many of you know
Gave up the ghost at half past nine.
That evening he had been to dine
At Gressington's—an act unwise,
But not the cause of his demise.
The doctors all agree that he
Was touched with cardiac atrophy
Accelerated (more or less)
By lack of proper food, distress,
Uncleanliness, and loss of sleep.

   He was a man that could not keep
His money (when he had the same)
Because of creditors who came
And took it from him; and he gave
So freely that he could not save.

   But all the while a sort of whim
Persistently remained with him,
Half admirable, half absurd:
To keep his word, to keep his word. . . .
By which he did not mean what you
And I would mean (of payments due
Or punctual rental of the Flat—
He was a deal too mad for that)

But—as he put it with a fine
Abandon, foolish or divine—
But " That great word which every man
Gave God before his life began."
It was a sacred word, he said,
Which comforted the pathless dead
And made God smile when it was shown
Unforfeited, before the Throne.
And this (he said) he meant to hold
In spite of debt, and hate, and cold;
And this (he said) he meant to show
As passport to the Wards below.
He boasted of it and gave praise
To his own self through all his days.

He wrote a record to preserve
How steadfastly he did not swerve
From keeping it; how stiff he stood
Its guardian, and maintained it good.
He had two witnesses to swear
He kept it once in Berkeley Square.
(Where hardly anything survives)
And, through the loneliest of lives
He kept it clean, he kept it still,
Down to the last extremes of ill.

So when he died, of many friends
Who came in crowds from all the ends
Of London, that it might be known
They knew the man who died alone,

THE FANATIC

Some, who had thought his mood sublime
And sent him soup from time to time,
Said, " Well, you cannot make them fit
The world, and there's an end of it ! "
But others, wondering at him, said :
" The man that kept his word is dead ! "
   Then angrily, a certain third
Cried, " Gentlemen, he kept his word.
And as a man whom beasts surround
Tumultuous, on a little mound
Stands Archer, for one dreadful hour,
Because a Man is born to Power—
And still, to daunt the pack below,
Twangs the clear purpose of his bow,
Till overwhelmed he dares to fall :
So stood this bulwark of us all.
He kept his word as none but he
Could keep it, and as did not we.
And round him as he kept his word
To-day's diseased and faithless herd,
A moment loud, a moment strong,
But foul forever, rolled along."

THE EARLY MORNING

THE moon on the one hand, the dawn on the other:
The moon is my sister, the dawn is my brother.
The moon on my left and the dawn on my right.
My brother, good morning: my sister, good night.

OUR LORD AND OUR LADY

THEY warned Our Lady for the Child
  That was Our blessed Lord,
And She took Him into the desert wild,
  Over the camel's ford.

And a long song She sang to Him
  And a short story told:
And She wrapped Him in a woollen cloak
  To keep Him from the cold.

But when Our Lord was grown a man
  The Rich they dragged Him down,
And they crucified Him in Golgotha,
  Out and beyond the Town.

They crucified Him on Calvary,
  Upon an April day;
And because He had been her little Son
  She followed Him all the way.

Our Lady stood beside the Cross,
  A little space apart,
And when She heard Our Lord cry out
  A sword went through Her Heart.

OUR LORD AND OUR LADY

They laid Our Lord in a marble tomb,
Dead, in a winding sheet.
But Our Lady stands above the world
With the white Moon at Her feet.

COURTESY

Of Courtesy, it is much less
Than Courage of Heart or Holiness,
Yet in my Walks it seems to me
That the Grace of God is in Courtesy.

On Monks I did in Storrington fall,
They took me straight into their Hall;
I saw Three Pictures on a wall,
And Courtesy was in them all.

The first the Annunciation;
The second the Visitation;
The third the Consolation,
Of God that was Our Lady's Son.

The first was of Saint Gabriel;
On Wings a-flame from Heaven he fell;
And as he went upon one knee
He shone with Heavenly Courtesy.

Our Lady out of Nazareth rode—
It was Her month of heavy load;
Yet was Her face both great and kind,
For Courtesy was in Her Mind.

COURTESY

The third it was our Little Lord,
Whom all the Kings in arms adored;
He was so small you could not see
His large intent of Courtesy.

Our Lord, that was Our Lady's Son,
Go bless you, People, one by one;
My Rhyme is written, my work is done.

THE NIGHT

Most holy Night, that still dost keep
The keys of all the doors of sleep,
To me when my tired eyelids close
    Give thou repose.

And let the far lament of them
That chaunt the dead day's requiem
Make in my ears, who wakeful lie,
    Soft lullaby.

Let them that guard the horned moon
By my bedside their memories croon.
So shall I have new dreams and blest
    In my brief rest.

Fold your great wings about my face,
Hide dawning from my resting-place,
And cheat me with your false delight,
    Most Holy Night.

THE LEADER

THE sword fell down: I heard a knell;
    I thought that ease was best,
And sullen men that buy and sell
    Were host: and I was guest.
All unashamed I sat with swine,
    We shook the dice for war,
The night was drunk with an evil wine—
    But she went on before.

> *She rode a steed of the sea-foam breed,*
>   *All faery was her blade,*
> *And the armour on her tender limbs*
>   *Was of the moonshine made.*

By God that sends the master-maids,
    I know not whence she came,
But the sword she bore to save the soul
    Went up like an altar flame
Where a broken race in a desert place
    Call on the Holy Name.

> *We strained our eyes in the dim day-rise,*
>   *We could not see them plain;*

THE LEADER

But two dead men from Valmy fen
Rode at her bridle-rein.

I hear them all, my fathers call,
  I see them how they ride,
And where had been that rout obscene
  Was an army straight with pride.
A hundred thousand marching men,
  Of squadrons twenty score,
And after them all the guns, the guns,
  But she went on before.

  Her face was like a king's command
  When all the swords are drawn.
  She stretched her arms and smiled at us,
  Her head was higher than the hills.
  She led us to the endless plains.
  We lost her in the dawn.

A BIVOUAC

I

You came without a human sound,
  You came and brought my soul to me;
I only woke, and all around
They slumbered on the firelit ground,
  Beside the guns in Burgundy.

II

I felt the gesture of your hands,
  You signed my forehead with the Cross;
The gesture of your holy hands
Was bounteous—like the misty lands
  Along the Hills in Calvados.

III

But when I slept I saw your eyes,
  Hungry as death, and very far.
I saw demand in your dim eyes
Mysterious as the moons that rise
  At midnight, in the Pines of Var.

TO THE BALLIOL MEN STILL IN AFRICA

YEARS ago when I was at Balliol,
  Balliol men—and I was one—
Swam together in winter rivers,
  Wrestled together under the sun.
And still in the heart of us, Balliol, Balliol,
  Loved already, but hardly known,
Welded us each of us into the others:
  Called a levy and chose her own.

Here is a House that armours a man
  With the eyes of a boy and the heart of a ranger,
And a laughing way in the teeth of the world
  And a holy hunger and thirst for danger:
Balliol made me, Balliol fed me,
  Whatever I had she gave me again:
And the best of Balliol loved and led me.
  God be with you, Balliol men.

I have said it before, and I say it again,
  There was treason done, and a false word spoken,
And England under the dregs of men,
  And bribes about, and a treaty broken:

TO THE BALLIOL MEN STILL IN AFRICA

But angry, lonely, hating it still,
 I wished to be there in spite of the wrong.
My heart was heavy for Cumnor Hill
 And the hammer of galloping all day long.

Galloping outward into the weather,
 Hands a-ready and battle in all :
Words together and wine together
 And song together in Balliol Hall.
Rare and single !   Noble and few ! . . .
 Oh ! they have wasted you over the sea !
The only brothers ever I knew,
 The men that laughed and quarrelled with me.

   • • • • • •

Balliol made me, Balliol fed me,
 Whatever I had she gave me again ;
And the best of Balliol loved and led me,
 God be with you, Balliol men.

VERSES TO A LORD WHO, IN THE HOUSE OF LORDS, SAID THAT THOSE WHO OPPOSED THE SOUTH AFRICAN AD-VENTURE CONFUSED SOLDIERS WITH MONEY-GRUBBERS

You thought because we held, my lord,
    An ancient cause and strong,
That therefore we maligned the sword:
    My lord, you did us wrong.

We also know the sacred height
    Up on Tugela side,
Where those three hundred fought with Beit
    And fair young Wernher died.

The daybreak on the failing force,
    The final sabres drawn:
Tall Goltman, silent on his horse,
    Superb against the dawn.

The little mound where Eckstein stood
    And gallant Albu fell,
And Oppenheim, half blind with blood
Went fording through the rising flood—
    My Lord, we know them well.

VERSES TO A LORD

The little empty homes forlorn,
The ruined synagogues that mourn,
  In Frankfort and Berlin;
We knew them when the peace was torn—
We of a nobler lineage born—
And now by all the gods of scorn
  We mean to rub them in.

THE REBEL

THERE is a wall of which the stones
Are lies and bribes and dead men's bones.
And wrongfully this evil wall
Denies what all men made for all,
And shamelessly this wall surrounds
Our homesteads and our native grounds.

But I will gather and I will ride,
And I will summon a countryside,
And many a man shall hear my halloa
Who never had thought the horn to follow;
And many a man shall ride with me
Who never had thought on earth to see
High Justice in her armoury.

When we find them where they stand,
A mile of men on either hand,
I mean to charge from right away
And force the flanks of their array,
And press them inward from the plains,
And drive them clamouring down the lanes,

THE REBEL

And gallop and harry and have them down,
And carry the gates and hold the town.
Then shall I rest me from my ride
With my great anger satisfied.

Only, before I eat and drink,
When I have killed them all, I think
That I will batter their carven names,
And slit the pictures in their frames,
And burn for scent their cedar door,
And melt the gold their women wore,
And hack their horses at the knees,
And hew to death their timber trees,
And plough their gardens deep and through—
And all these things I mean to do
For fear perhaps my little son
Should break his hands, as I have done.

THE PROPHET LOST IN THE HILLS
AT EVENING

STRONG God which made the topmost stars
  To circulate and keep their course,
Remember me; whom all the bars
  Of sense and dreadful fate enforce.

Above me in your heights and tall,
  Impassable the summits freeze,
Below the haunted waters call
  Impassable beyond the trees.

I hunger and I have no bread.
  My gourd is empty of the wine.
Surely the footsteps of the dead
  Are shuffling softly close to mine!

It darkens. I have lost the ford.
  There is a change on all things made.
The rocks have evil faces, Lord,
  And I am awfully afraid.

Remember me: The Voids of Hell
  Expand enormous all around.

THE PROPHET LOST IN THE HILLS

Strong friend of souls, Emmanuel,
    Redeem me from accursed ground.

The long descent of wasted days,
    To these at last have led me down;
Remember that I filled with praise
The meaningless and doubtful ways
    That lead to an eternal town.

I challenged and I kept the Faith,
    The bleeding path alone I trod;
It darkens.   Stand about my wraith,
    And harbour me—almighty God.

THE END OF THE ROAD

IN THESE BOOTS AND WITH THIS STAFF
Two hundred leaguers and a half
Walked I, went I, paced I, tripped I,
Marched I, held I, skelped I, slipped I,
Pushed I, panted, swung and dashed I ;
Picked I, forded, swam and splashed I,
Strolled I, climbed I, crawled and scrambled,
Dropped and dipped I, ranged and rambled ;
Plodded I, hobbled I, trudged and tramped I,
And in lonely spinnies camped I,
And in haunted pinewoods slept I,
Lingered, loitered, limped and crept I,
Clambered, halted, stepped and leapt I ;
Slowly sauntered, roundly strode I,
And . . .　　　(Oh ! Patron saints and Angels
　　　　　That protect the four Evangels !
　　　　　And you Prophets vel majores
　　　　　Vel incerti, vel minores,
　　　　　Virgines ac confessores
　　　　　Chief of whose peculiar glories
　　　　　Est in Aula Regis stare
　　　　　Atque orare et exorare
　　　　　Et clamare et conclamare
71

THE END OF THE ROAD

Clamantes cum clamoribus
Pro Nobis Peccatoribus.)
Let me not conceal it. . . . *Rode I.*
(For who but critics could complain
Of " riding " in a railway train ?)
Across the valleys and the high-land,
With all the world on either hand
Drinking when I had a mind to,
Singing when I felt inclined to ;
Nor ever turned my face to home
Till I had slaked my heart at Rome.

AN ORACLE

THAT WARNED THE WRITER WHEN ON PILGRIMAGE

MATUTINUS adest ubi Vesper, et accipiens te
Saepe recusatum voces intelligit hospes
Rusticus ignotas notas, ac flumina tellus
Occupat—In sancto tum, tum, stans Aede caveto
Tonsuram Hirsuti Capitis, via namque pedestrem
Ferrea praeveniens cursum, peregrine, laborem
Pro pietate tua inceptum frustratur, amore
Antiqui Ritus alto sub Numine Romae.

Translation of the above :—

When early morning seems but eve
And they that still refuse receive :
When speech unknown men understand ;
And floods are crossed upon dry land.
Within the Sacred Walls beware
The Shaven Head that boasts of Hair,
For when the road attains the rail
The Pilgrim's great attempt shall fail.

THE DEATH AND LAST CONFESSION OF
WANDERING PETER

WHEN Peter Wanderwide was young
    He wandered everywhere he would:
And all that he approved was sung,
    And most of what he saw was good.

When Peter Wanderwide was thrown
    By Death himself beyond Auxerre,
He chanted in heroic tone
    To priests and people gathered there:

'If all that I have loved and seen
    Be with me on the Judgment Day,
I shall be saved the crowd between
    From Satan and his foul array.

"Almighty God will surely cry,
    'St Michael! Who is this that stands
With Ireland in his dubious eye,
    And Perigord between his hands,

"'And on his arm the stirrup-thongs,
    And in his gait the narrow seas,

THE DEATH OF PETER

And in his mouth Burgundian songs,
    But in his heart the Pyrenees ? '

" St Michael then will answer right
    (And not without angelic shame),
' I seem to know his face by sight :
    I cannot recollect his name . . . ? '

" St Peter will befriend me then,
    Because my name is Peter too :
' I know him for the best of men
    That ever wallopped barley brew.

" ' And though I did not know him well
    And though his soul were clogged with sin,
I hold the keys of Heaven and Hell.
    Be welcome, noble Peterkin.'

" Then shall I spread my native wings
    And tread secure the heavenly floor,
And tell the Blessed doubtful things
    Of Val d'Aran and Perigord."

This was the last and solemn jest
    Of weary Peter Wanderwide.
He spoke it with a failing zest,
    And having spoken it, he died.

DEDICATORY ODE

I MEAN to write with all my strength
  (It lately has been sadly waning),
A ballad of enormous length—
  Some parts of which will need explaining.[1]

Because (unlike the bulk of men
  Who write for fame or public ends),
I turn a lax and fluent pen
  To talking of my private friends.[2]

For no one, in our long decline,
  So dusty, spiteful and divided,
Had quite such pleasant friends as mine,
  Or loved them half as much as I did.

·   ·   ·   ·   ·   ·   ·

[1] But do not think I shall explain
    To any great extent.   Believe me,
  I partly write to give you pain,
    And if you do not like me, leave me.

[2] And least of all can you complain,
    Reviewers, whose unholy trade is,
  To puff with all your might and main
    Biographies of single ladies.

76

DEDICATORY ODE

The Freshman ambles down the High,
  In love with everything he sees,
He notes the racing autumn sky,
  He sniffs a lively autumn breeze.

" Can this be Oxford ?   This the place ? "
  (He cries) " of which my father said
The tutoring was a damned disgrace,
  The creed a mummery, stuffed and dead ?

" Can it be here that Uncle Paul
  Was driven by excessive gloom,
To drink and debt, and, last of all,
  To smoking opium in his room ?

" Is it from here the people come,
  Who talk so loud, and roll their eyes,
And stammer ?   How extremely rum !
  How curious !   What a great surprise !

" Some influence of a nobler day
  Than theirs (I mean than Uncle Paul's),
Has roused the sleep of their decay,
  And flecked with light their crumbling walls.

" O ! dear undaunted boys of old,
  Would that your names were carven here,
For all the world in stamps of gold,
  That I might read them and revere.

DEDICATORY ODE

" Who wrought and handed down for me
 This Oxford of the larger air,
Laughing, and full of faith, and free,
 With youth resplendent everywhere ? "

Then learn : thou ill-instructed, blind,
 Young, callow, and untutored man,
Their private names were . . . .[1]
 Their club was called REPUBLICAN.

 . . . . . .

Where on their banks of light they lie,
 The happy hills of Heaven between,
The Gods that rule the morning sky
 Are not more young, nor more serene

Than were the intrepid Four that stand,
 The first who dared to live their dream.
And on this uncongenial land
 To found the Abbey of Theleme.

We kept the Rabelaisian plan :[2]
 We dignified the dainty cloisters

----

[1] Never mind.

[2] The plan forgot (I know not how,
 Perhaps the Refectory filled it),
To put a chapel in ; and now
 We're mortgaging the rest to build it.

DEDICATORY ODE

With Natural Law, the Rights of Man,
  Song, Stoicism, Wine and Oysters.

The library was most inviting:
  The books upon the crowded shelves
Were mainly of our private writing:
  We kept a school and taught ourselves.

We taught the art of writing things
  On men we still should like to throttle:
And where to get the Blood of Kings
  At only half a crown a bottle.

　·　　·　　·　　·　　·　　·

Eheu Fugaces! Postume!
  (An old quotation out of mode);
My coat of dreams is stolen away
  My youth is passing down the road.

　·　　·　　·　　·　　·　　·

The wealth of youth, we spent it well
  And decently, as very few can.
And is it lost?   I cannot tell:
  And what is more, I doubt if you can.

The question's very much too wide,
  And much too deep, and much too hollow,
And learned men on either side
  Use arguments I cannot follow.

DEDICATORY ODE

They say that in the unchanging place,
   Where all we loved is always dear,
We meet our morning face to face
   And find at last our twentieth year. . . .

They say (and I am glad they say)
   It is so; and it may be so:
It may be just the other way,
   I cannot tell. But this I know:

From quiet homes and first beginning,
   Out to the undiscoveréd ends,
There's nothing worth the wear of winning,
   But laughter and the love of friends.

.   .   .   .   .   .

But something dwindles, oh! my peers,
   And something cheats the heart and passes,
And Tom that meant to shake the years
   Has come to merely rattling glasses.

And He, the Father of the Flock,
   Is keeping Burmesans in order,
An exile on a lonely rock
   That overlooks the Chinese border.

And One (Myself I mean—no less),
   Ah!—will Posterity believe it—

DEDICATORY ODE

Not only don't deserve success,
    But hasn't managed to achieve it.

Not even this peculiar town
    Has ever fixed a friendship firmer,
But—one is married, one's gone down,
    And one's a Don, and one's in Burmah.

   .   .   .   .

And oh! the days, the days, the days,
    When all the four were off together:
The infinite deep of summer haze,
    The roaring boast of autumn weather!

   .   .   .   .

I will not try the reach again,
    I will not set my sail alone,
To moor a boat bereft of men
    At Yarnton's tiny docks of stone.

But I will sit beside the fire,
    And put my hand before my eyes,
And trace, to fill my heart's desire,
    The last of all our Odysseys.

The quiet evening kept her tryst:
    Beneath an open sky we rode,
And passed into a wandering mist
    Along the perfect Evenlode.

DEDICATORY ODE

The tender Evenlode that makes
   Her meadows hush to hear the sound
Of waters mingling in the brakes,
   And binds my heart to English ground.

A lovely river, all alone,
   She lingers in the hills and holds
A hundred little towns of stone,
   Forgotten in the western wolds.

.   .   .   .   .   .

I dare to think (though meaner powers
   Possess our thrones, and lesser wits
Are drinking worser wine than ours,
   In what's no longer Austerlitz)

That surely a tremendous ghost,
   The brazen-lunged, the bumper-filler,
Still sings to an immortal toast,
   The Misadventures of the Miller.

The unending seas are hardly bar
   To men with such a prepossession :
We were ?   Why then, by God, we *are*—
   Order !   I call the Club to session !

You do retain the song we set,
   And how it rises, trips and scans ?
You keep the sacred memory yet,
   Republicans ?   Republicans ?

DEDICATORY ODE

You know the way the words were hurled,
    To break the worst of fortune's rub ?
I give the toast across the world,
    And drink it, " Gentlemen : the Club."

DEDICATION ON THE GIFT OF A BOOK
TO A CHILD

CHILD ! do not throw this book about !
    Refrain from the unholy pleasure
Of cutting all the pictures out !
    Preserve it as your chiefest treasure.

Child, have you never heard it said
    That you are heir to all the ages ?
Why, then, your hands were never made
    To tear these beautiful thick pages !

Your little hands were made to take
    The better things and leave the worse ones :
They also may be used to shake
    The Massive Paws of Elder Persons.

And when your prayers complete the day,
    Darling, your little tiny hands
Were also made, I think, to pray
    For men that lose their fairylands.

DEDICATION OF A CHILD'S BOOK OF IMAGINARY TALES

WHEREIN WRONG-DOERS SUFFER

AND is it true ? It is not true !
And if it was it wouldn't do
For people such as me and you,
Who very nearly all day long
Are doing something rather wrong.

85

HOMAGE

I

THERE is a light around your head
Which only Saints of God may wear,
And all the flowers on which you tread
In pleasaunce more than ours have fed,
And supped the essential air
Whose summer is a-pulse with music everywhere.

II

For you are younger than the mornings are
That in the mountains break;
When upland shepherds see their only star
Pale on the dawn, and make
In his surcease the hours,
The early hours of all their happy circuit take.

THE MOON'S FUNERAL

I

THE Moon is dead.   I saw her die.
She in a drifting cloud was drest,
She lay along the uncertain west,
A dream to see.
And very low she spake to me:
" I go where none may understand,
I fade into the nameless land,
And there must lie perpetually."
And therefore I,
And therefore loudly, loudly I
And high
And very piteously make cry:
" The Moon is dead.   I saw her die."

II

And will she never rise again ?
The Holy Moon ?   Oh, never more !
Perhaps along the inhuman shore
Where pale ghosts are

THE MOON'S FUNERAL

Beyond the low lethean fen
She and some wide infernal star . . .
To us who loved her never more,
The Moon will never rise again.
Oh! never more in nightly sky
Her eye so high shall peep and pry
To see the great world rolling by.
For why?
The Moon is dead.   I saw her die.

THE HAPPY JOURNALIST

I LOVE to walk about at night
　　By nasty lanes and corners foul,
All shielded from the unfriendly light
　　And independent as the owl.

By dirty grates I love to lurk ;
　　I often stoop to take a squint
At printers working at their work.
　　I muse upon the rot they print.

The beggars please me, and the mud :
　　The editors beneath their lamps
As—Mr Howl demanding blood,
　　And Lord Retender stealing stamps,

And Mr Bing instructing liars,
　　His elder son composing trash ;
Beaufort (whose real name is Meyers)
　　Refusing anything but cash.

I like to think of Mr Meyers,
　　I like to think of Mr Bing.
I like to think about the liars :
　　It pleases me, that sort of thing.

THE HAPPY JOURNALIST

Policemen speak to me, but I,
    Remembering my civic rights,
Neglect them and do not reply.
    I love to walk about at nights!

At twenty-five to four I bunch
    Across a cab I can't afford.
I ring for breakfast after lunch.
    I am as happy as a lord!

LINES TO A DON

REMOTE and ineffectual Don
That dared attack my Chesterton,
With that poor weapon, half-impelled,
Unlearnt, unsteady, hardly held,
Unworthy for a tilt with men—
Your quavering and corroded pen;
Don poor at Bed and worse at Table,
Don pinched, Don starved, Don miserable;
Don stuttering, Don with roving eyes,
Don nervous, Don of crudities;
Don clerical, Don ordinary,
Don self-absorbed and solitary;
Don here-and-there, Don epileptic;
Don puffed and empty, Don dyspeptic;
Don middle-class, Don sycophantic,
Don dull, Don brutish, Don pedantic;
Don hypocritical, Don bad,
Don furtive, Don three-quarters mad;
Don (since a man must make an end),
Don that shall never be my friend.

.   .   .   .   .   .

Don different from those regal Dons!
With hearts of gold and lungs of bronze,

91

LINES TO A DON

Who shout and bang and roar and bawl
The Absolute across the hall ,
Or sail in amply bellying gown
Enormous through the Sacred Town,
Bearing from College to their homes
Deep cargoes of gigantic tomes ;
Dons admirable ! Dons of Might !
Uprising on my inward sight
Compact of ancient tales, and port
And sleep—and learning of a sort.
Dons English, worthy of the land ;
Dons rooted ; Dons that understand.
Good Dons perpetual that remain
A landmark, walling in the plain—
The horizon of my memories—
Like large and comfortable trees.

  .   .   .   .   .   .

Don very much apart from these,
Thou scapegoat Don, thou Don devoted,
Don to thine own damnation quoted,
Perplexed to find thy trivial name
Reared in my verse to lasting shame.
Don dreadful, rasping Don and wearing,
Repulsive Don—Don past all bearing.
Don of the cold and doubtful breath,
Don despicable, Don of death ;
Don nasty, skimpy, silent, level ;
Don evil ; Don that serves the devil.

LINES TO A DON

Don ugly—that makes fifty lines.
There is a Canon which confines
A Rhymed Octosyllabic Curse
If written in Iambic Verse
To fifty lines.   I never cut;
I far prefer to end it—but
Believe me I shall soon return.
My fires are banked, but still they burn
To write some more about the Don
That dared attack my Chesterton.

NEWDIGATE POEM

A PRIZE POEM SUBMITTED BY MR LAMBKIN, THEN SCHOLAR AND LATER FELLOW OF BURFORD COLLEGE, TO THE EXAMINERS OF THE UNIVERSITY OF OXFORD ON THE PRESCRIBED POETIC THEME SET BY THEM IN 1893, "THE BENEFITS OF THE ELECTRIC LIGHT"

HAIL, Happy Muse, and touch the tuneful string !
The benefits conferred by Science [1] I sing.
Under the kind Examiners' direction [2]
I only write about them in connection
With benefits which the Electric Light
Confers on us ; especially at night.
These are my theme, of these my song shall rise.
My lofty head shall swell to strike the skies.[3]
And tears of hopeless love bedew the maiden's eyes.
Descend, O Muse, from thy divine abode,
To Osney, on the Seven Bridges Road ;
For under Osney's solitary shade
The bulk of the Electric Light is made.
Here are the works ;—from hence the current flows
Which (so the Company's prospectus goes)

[1] To be pronounced as a monosyllable in the Imperial fashion.
[2] Mr Punt, Mr Howl, and Mr Grewcock (now, alas, deceased).
[3] A neat rendering of " Sublimi feriam sidera vertice."

94

NEWDIGATE POEM

Can furnish to Subscribers hour by hour
No less than sixteen thousand candle power,[1]
All at a thousand volts.   (It is essential
To keep the current at this high potential
In spite of the considerable expense.)
The Energy developed represents,
Expressed in foot-tons, the united forces
Of fifteen elephants and forty horses.
But shall my scientific detail thus
Clip the dear wings of Buoyant Pegasus ?
Shall pure statistics jar upon the ear
That pants for Lyric accents loud and clear ?
Shall I describe the complex Dynamo
Or write about its Commutator ?   No !
To happier fields I lead my wanton pen,
The proper study of mankind is men.
Awake, my Muse !   Portray the pleasing sight
That meets us where they make Electric Light.
Behold the Electrician where he stands :
Soot, oil, and verdigris are on his hands ;
Large spots of grease defile his dirty clothes,
The while his conversation drips with oaths.
Shall such a being perish in its youth ?
Alas ! it is indeed the fatal truth.
In that dull brain, beneath that hair unkempt,
Familiarity has bred contempt.

[1] To the Examiners : These facts (of which I guarantee the accuracy) were given me by a Director.

We warn him of the gesture all too late :
Oh, Heartless Jove ! Oh, Adamantine Fate !
    A random touch—a hand's imprudent slip—
The Terminals—a flash—a sound like " Zip ! "
A smell of burning fills the started Air—
The Electrician is no longer there !
    But let us turn with true Artistic scorn
From facts funereal and from views forlorn
Of Erebus and Blackest midnight born.[1]
    Arouse thee, Muse ! and chaunt in accents rich
The interesting processes by which
The Electricity is passed along :
These are my theme : to these I bend my song.
    It runs encased in wood or porous brick
Through copper wires two millimetres thick,
And insulated on their dangerous mission
By indiarubber, silk, or composition.
Here you may put with critical felicity
The following question : " What is Electricity ? "
    " Molecular Activity," say some,
Others when asked say nothing, and are dumb.
Whatever be its nature, this is clear :
The rapid current checked in its career,
Baulked in its race and halted in its course [2]
Transforms to heat and light its latent force :

[1] A reminiscence of Milton : " Fas est et ab hoste docere."

[2] Lambkin told me he regretted this line, which was for the sake of Rhyme. He would willingly have replaced it, but to his last day could construct no substitute.

96

NEWDIGATE POEM

It needs no pedant in the lecturer's chair
To prove that light and heat are present there.
The pear-shaped vacuum globe, I understand,
Is far too hot to fondle with the hand.
While, as is patent to the meanest sight,
The carbon filament is very bright.

As for the lights they hang about the town,
Some praise them highly, others run them down.
This system (technically called the Arc),
Makes some passages too light, others too dark.

But in the house the soft and constant rays
Have always met with universal praise.

For instance: if you want to read in bed
No candle burns beside your curtain's head,
Far from some distant corner of the room
The incandescent lamp dispels the gloom,
And with the largest print need hardly try
The powers of any young and vigorous eye.

Aroint thee, Muse! Inspired the poet sings!
I cannot help observing future things!
Life is a vale, its paths are dark and rough
Only because we do not know enough:
When Science has discovered something more
We shall be happier than we were before.

Hail, Britain, Mistress of the Azure Main,
Ten thousand Fleets swoop over thee in vain!
Hail, Mighty Mother of the Brave and Free,
That beat Napoleon, and gave birth to me!

NEWDIGATE POEM

Thou that canst wrap in thine emblazoned robe
One quarter of the habitable globe.
Thy mountains, wafted by a favouring breeze,
Like mighty rocks withstand the stormy seas.
    Thou art a Christian Commonwealth; and yet
Be thou not all unthankful—nor forget
As thou exultest in Imperial Might
The Benefits of the Electric Light.

THE YELLOW MUSTARD

Oh! ye that prink it to and fro,
In pointed flounce and furbelow,
What have ye known, what can ye know
That have not seen the mustard grow?

The yellow mustard is no less
Than God's good gift to loneliness;
And he was sent in gorgeous press
To jangle keys at my distress.

I heard the throstle call again,
Come hither, Pain! come hither, Pain!
Till all my shameless feet were fain
To wander through the summer rain.

And far apart from human place,
And flaming like a vast disgrace,
There struck me blinding in the face
The livery of the mustard race.

. . . . . .

To see the yellow mustard grow
Beyond the town, above, below;
Beyond the purple houses, oh!
To see the yellow mustard grow!

THE POLITICIAN
OR THE IRISH EARLDOM

A STRONG and striking Personality,
    Worth several hundred thousand pounds—
Of strict political Morality—
    Was walking in his park-like Grounds;
When, just as these began to pall on him
    (I mean the Trees, and Things like that),
A Person who had come to call on him
    Approached him, taking off his Hat.

He said, with singular veracity:
    " I serve our Sea-girt Mother-Land
In no conspicuous capacity.
    I am but an Attorney; and
I do a little elementary
    Negotiation, now and then,
As Agent for a Parliamentary
    Division of the Town of N. . . .

" Merely as one of the Electorate—
    A member of the Commonweal—
Before completing my Directorate,
    I want to know the way you feel

THE POLITICIAN

On matters more or less debatable;
  As—whether our Imperial Pride
Can treat as taxable or rateable
  The Gardens of . . ." His host replied:

"The Ravages of Inebriety
  (Alas! increasing day by day!)
Are undermining all Society.
  I do not hesitate to say
My country squanders her abilities,
  Observe how Montenegro treats
Her Educational Facilities. . . .
  . . . As to the African defeats,

" I bitterly deplored their frequency;
  On Canada we are agreed,
The Laws protecting Public Decency
  Are very, very lax indeed!
The Views of most of the Nobility
  Are very much the same as mine,
On Thingumbob's eligibility . . .
  I trust that you remain to dine ? "

His Lordship pressed with importunity,
  As rarely he had pressed before.

•   •   •   •   •   •

It gave them both an opportunity
  To know each other's value more.

101

THE LOSER

HE lost his money first of all
   —And losing that is half the story—
And later on he tried a fall
   With Fate, in things less transitory.

He lost his heart—and found it dead—
   (His one and only true discovery),
And after that he lost his head,
   And lost his chances of recovery.

He lost his honour bit by bit
   Until the thing was out of question.
He worried so at losing it,
   He lost his sleep and his digestion.

He lost his temper—and for good—
   The remnants of his reputation,
His taste in wine, his choice of food,
   And then, in rapid culmination,

His certitudes, his sense of truth,
   His memory, his self-control,
The love that graced his early youth,
   And lastly his immortal soul.

TWELFTH NIGHT

As I was lifting over Down
A winter's night to Petworth Town,
I came upon a company
Of Travellers who would talk with me.

The riding moon was small and bright,
They cast no shadows in her light:
There was no man for miles a-near.
I would not walk with them for fear.

A star in heaven by Gumber glowed,
An ox across the darkness lowed,
Whereat a burning light there stood
Right in the heart of Gumber Wood.

Across the rime their marching rang,
And in a little while they sang;
They sang a song I used to know,
                    Gloria
In Excelsis Domino.

The frozen way those people trod
It led towards the Mother of God;
Perhaps if I had travelled with them
I might have come to Bethlehem.

103

THE SEASONS

They whom their mothers bare through Summer heat,
Are boys of Autumn, and a fruit complete.

They whom their mothers bare through April rain,
Are new as April, and as April vain.

They whom their mothers in dark Winters bare,
Wake to a barren world, and straight despair.

But they that held through Winter to the Spring
Despair as I do, and, as I do, sing.

DOWN CHANNEL

The Channel pours out on the Ebb in a river gigantic.
   There is no Moon.
The Dark is low in a cloud on the huge Atlantic.
   We'll be raising the Lizard soon.

There will be no meeting of eyes, nor any blessing,
   After the run.
The lips are still and the hand has ceased from
      caressing.
   There is nothing more to be done.

III
SONGS

NOËL

On a winter's night long time ago
 (*The bells ring loud and the bells ring low*),
When high howled wind, and down fell snow
 (Carillon, Carilla).
Saint Joseph he and Nostre Dame,
Riding on an ass, full weary came
From Nazareth into Bethlehem.
  And the small child Jesus smile on you.

II

And Bethlehem inn they stood before
 (*The bells ring less and the bells ring more*),
The landlord bade them begone from his door
 (Carillon, Carilla).
" Poor folk " (says he), " must lie where they may,
For the Duke of Jewry comes this way,
With all his train on a Christmas Day."
  And the small child Jesus smile on you.

NOËL

III

Poor folk that may my carol hear
    (*The bells ring single and the bells ring clear*),
See!   God's one child had hardest cheer!
    (Carillon, Carilla).
Men grown hard on a Christmas morn;
The dumb beast by and a babe forlorn.
It was very, very cold when our Lord was born.
    And the small child Jesus smile on you.

IV

Now these were Jews as Jews must be
    (*The bells ring merry and the bells ring free*).
But Christian men in a band are we
    (Carillon, Carilla).
Empty we go, and ill be-dight,
Singing Noël on a Winter's night.
Give us to sup by the warm firelight,
    And the small child Jesus smile on you.

THE BIRDS

WHEN Jesus Christ was four years old,
The angels brought Him toys of gold,
Which no man ever had bought or sold.

And yet with these He would not play.
He made Him small fowl out of clay,
And blessed them till they flew away:
  Tu creasti Domine.

Jesus Christ, Thou child so wise,
Bless mine hands and fill mine eyes,
And bring my soul to Paradise.

IN A BOAT

LADY! Lady!
Upon Heaven-height,
Above the harsh morning
In the mere light.

Above the spindrift
And above the snow,
Where no seas tumble,
And no winds blow.

The twisting tides,
And the perilous sands
Upon all sides
Are in your holy hands.

The wind harries
And the cold kills;
But I see your chapel
Over far hills.

My body is frozen,
My soul is afraid:
Stretch out your hands to me,
Mother and maid.

112

IN A BOAT

Mother of Christ,
And Mother of me,
Save me alive
From the howl of the sea.

If you will Mother me
Till I grow old,
I will hang in your chapel
A ship of pure gold.

SONG

INVITING THE INFLUENCE OF A YOUNG LADY
UPON THE OPENING YEAR

I

You wear the morning like your dress
And are with mastery crowned;
Whenas you walk your loveliness
Goes shining all around.
Upon your secret, smiling way
Such new contents were found,
The Dancing Loves made holiday
On that delighted ground.

II

Then summon April forth, and send
Commandment through the flowers;
About our woods your grace extend
A queen of careless hours.
For oh, not Vera veiled in rain,
Nor Dian's sacred Ring,
With all her royal nymphs in train
Could so lead on the Spring.

THE RING

Wʜᴇɴ I was flying before the King
In the wood of Valognes in my hiding,
Although I had not anything
I sent a woman a golden ring.

A Ring of the Moors beyond Leon
With emerald and with diamond stone,
And a writing no man ever had known,
And an opal standing all alone.

The shape of the ring the heart to bind:
The emerald turns from cold to kind:
The writing makes her sure to find:—
But the evil opal changed her mind.

Now when the King was dead, was he,
I came back hurriedly over the sea
From the long rocks in Normandy
To Bosham that is by Selsey.
And we clipt each other knee to knee.
But what I had was lost to me.

CUCKOO!

In woods so long time bare.
    Cuckoo!
Up and in the wood, I know not where
Two notes fall.
Yet I do not envy him at all
His phantasy.
Cuckoo!
I too,
Somewhere,
I have sung as merrily as he
Who can dare,
Small and careless lover, so to laugh at care,
And who
Can call
Cuckoo!
In woods of winter weary,
In scented woods, of winter weary, call
Cuckoo!
In woods so long time bare.

116

THE LITTLE SERVING MAID

I

THERE was a Queen of England,
  And a good Queen too.
She had a house in Powis Land
  With the Severn running through;
And Men-folk and Women-folk
  Apprenticed to a trade;
But the prettiest of all
  Was a Little Serving Maid.

II

"Oh Madam, Queen of England!
  Oh will you let me go!
For there's a Lad in London
  And he would have it so.
And I would have it too, Madam,
  And with him would I bide;
And he will be the Groom, Madam,
  And I shall be the Bride!"

THE LITTLE SERVING MAID

III

" Oh fie to you and shame to you,
  You Little Serving Maid !
And are you not astonied ?
  And are you not afraid ?
For never was it known
  Since Yngelonde began
That a Little Serving Maid
  Should go a-meeting of a man !

IV

Then the Little Serving Maid
  She went and laid her down,
With her cross and her beads,
  In her new courting gown.
And she called in Mother Mary's name
  And heavily she sighed :
" I think that I have come to shame ! "
  And after that she died.

V

The good Queen of England
  Her women came and ran :
" The Little Serving Maid is dead
  From loving of a man ! "

118

THE LITTLE SERVING MAID

Said the good Queen of England
  " That is ill news to hear!
Take her out and shroud her,
  And lay her on a bier."

VI

They laid her on a bier,
  In the court-yard all;
Some came from Foresting,
  And some came from Hall.
And Great Lords carried her,
  And proud Priests prayed.
And that was the end
  Of the Little Serving Maid.

AUVERGNAT

THERE was a man was half a clown
   (It's so my father tells of it).
He saw the church in Clermont town
And laughed to hear the bells of it.

He laughed to hear the bells that ring
In Clermont Church and round of it;
He heard the verger's daughter sing,
And loved her for the sound of it.

The verger's daughter said him nay;
She had the right of choice in it.
He left the town at break of day:
He hadn't had a voice in it.

The road went up, the road went down,
And there the matter ended it.
He broke his heart in Clermont town,
At Pontgibaud they mended it.

DRINKING SONG

DRINKING SONG

ON THE EXCELLENCE OF BURGUNDY WINE

My jolly fat host with your face all a-grin,
Come, open the door to us, let us come in.
A score of stout fellows who think it no sin
If they toast till they're hoarse, and they drink till
   they spin,
      Hoofed it amain,
      Rain or no rain,
   To crack your old jokes, and your bottle to
      drain.

Such a warmth in the belly that nectar begets
As soon as his guts with its humour he wets,
The miser his gold, and the student his debts,
And the beggar his rags and his hunger forgets.
      For there's never a wine
      Like this tipple of thine
   From the great hill of Nuits to the River of
      Rhine.

Outside you may hear the great gusts as they go
By Foy, by Duerne, and the hills of Lerraulx,

DRINKING SONG

But the rain he may rain, and the wind he may blow,
If the Devil's above there's good liquor below.
      So it abound,
      Pass it around,
Burgundy's Burgundy all the year round.

DRINKING DIRGE

I put my pleasure ...

DRINKING DIRGE

A THOUSAND years ago I used to dine
   In houses where they gave me such regale
Of dear companionship and comrades fine
   That out I went alone beyond the pale;
And riding, laughed and dared the skies malign
   To show me all the undiscovered tale—
But my philosophy's no more divine,
   I put my pleasure in a pint of ale.

And you, my friends, oh! pleasant friends of mine,
   Who leave me now alone, without avail,
On Californian hills you gave me wine,
   You gave me cider-drink in Longuevaille;
If after many years you come to pine
   For comradeship that is an ancient tale—
You'll find me drinking beer in Dead Man's Chine.
   I put my pleasure in a pint of ale.

In many a briny boat I've tried the brine,
   From many a hidden harbour I've set sail,
Steering towards the sunset where there shine
   The distant amethystine islands pale.

123

DRINKING DIRGE

There are no ports beyond the far sea-line,
   Nor any halloa to meet the mariner's hail ;
I stand at home and slip the anchor-line.
   I put my pleasure in a pint of ale.

Envoi

Prince !   Is it true that when you go to dine
   You bring your bottle in a freezing pail ?
Why then you cannot be a friend of mine.
   I put my pleasure in a pint of ale.

WEST SUSSEX DRINKING SONG

THEY sell good Beer at Haslemere
  And under Guildford Hill.
At Little Cowfold as I've been told
  A beggar may drink his fill:
There is a good brew in Amberley too,
  And by the bridge also;
But the swipes they take in at Washington Inn
  Is the very best Beer I know.

Chorus

With my here it goes, there it goes,
  All the fun's before us:
The Tipple's Aboard and the night is young
The door's ajar and the Barrel is sprung,
I am singing the best song ever was sung
  And it has a rousing chorus.

If I were what I never can be,
  The master or the squire:
If you gave me the hundred from here to the sea,
  Which is more than I desire:

WEST SUSSEX DRINKING SONG

Then all my crops should be barley and hops,
  And did my harvest fail
I'd sell every rood of mine acres I would
  For a belly-full of good Ale.

Chorus

With my here it goes, there it goes,
  All the fun's before us:
The Tipple's aboard and the night is young,
The door's ajar and the Barrel is sprung,
I am singing the best song ever was sung
  And it has a rousing Chorus.

A BALLAD ON SOCIOLOGICAL ECONOMICS

A WHILE ago it came to pass
  (Merry we carol it all the day),
There sat a man on the top of an ass
  (Heart be happy and carol be gay
    In spite of the price of hay).

And over the down they hoofed it so
  (Happy go lucky has best of fare),
The man up above and the brute below
  (And singing we all forget to care
    A man may laugh if he dare).

Over the stubble and round the crop
  (Life is short and the world is round),
The donkey beneath and the man on the top
  (Oh! let good ale be found, be found,
    Merry good ale and sound).

It happened again as it happened before
  (Tobacco's a boon but ale is bliss),
The moke in the ditch and the man on the floor
  (And that is the moral to this, to this
    Remarkable artifice).

HERETICS ALL

HERETICS all, whoever you be,
In Tarbes or Nimes, or over the sea,
You never shall have good words from me.
  Caritas non conturbat me.

But Catholic men that live upon wine
Are deep in the water, and frank, and fine;
Wherever I travel I find it so,
  Benedicamus Domino.

On childing women that are forlorn,
And men that sweat in nothing but scorn:
That is on all that ever were born,
  Miserere Domine.

To my poor self on my deathbed,
And all my dear companions dead,
Because of the love that I bore them,
  Dona Eis Requiem.

HA'NACKER MILL

SALLY is gone that was so kindly
Sally is gone from Ha'nacker Hill.
And the Briar grows ever since then so blindly
    And ever since then the clapper is still,
    And the sweeps have fallen from Ha'nacker Mill.

Ha'nacker Hill is in Desolation :
    Ruin a-top and a field unploughed.
And Spirits that call on a fallen nation
    Spirits that loved her calling aloud :
    Spirits abroad in a windy cloud.

Spirits that call and no one answers ;
    Ha'nacker's down and England's done.
Wind and Thistle for pipe and dancers
    And never a ploughman under the Sun.
    Never a ploughman.   Never a one.

TARANTELLA

Do you remember an Inn,
Miranda ?
Do you remember an Inn ?
And the tedding and the spreading
Of the straw for a bedding,
And the fleas that tease in the High Pyrenees,
And the wine that tasted of the tar ?
And the cheers and the jeers of the young muleteers
(Under the vine of the dark verandah) ?
Do you remember an Inn, Miranda,
Do you remember an Inn ?
And the cheers and the jeers of the young muleteers
Who hadn't got a penny,
And who weren't paying any,
And the hammer at the doors and the Din ?
And the Hip ! Hop ! Hap !
Of the clap
Of the hands to the twirl and the swirl
Of the girl gone chancing,
Glancing,
Dancing,
Backing and advancing,
Snapping of a clapper to the spin

TARANTELLA

Out and in——
And the Ting, Tong, Tang of the Guitar !
Do you remember an Inn,
Miranda ?
Do you remember an Inn ?

Never more ;
Miranda,
Never more.
Only the high peaks hoar :
And Aragon a torrent at the door.
No sound
In the walls of the Halls where falls
The tread
Of the feet of the dead to the ground
No sound :
But the boom
Of the far Waterfall like Doom.

THE CHAUNTY OF THE " NONA "

I

COME list all ye Cullies and Doxies so dear,
You shall hearken to the tale of the Bold Marineer
That took ship out of Holyhead and drove her so
    hard
Past Bardsey, Pwlheli, Port Madoc, and Fishguard—
Past Bardsey, Pwlheli, Port Madoc, and Fishguard.

II

Then he dropped out of Fishguard on a calm
    Summer's day,
By St David's and Strumbles and across St Bride's
    Bay ;
Circumnavigating Skomer, that Island, around,
With the heart of a Lion he threaded Jack Sound—
With the heart of a Lion he threaded Jack Sound.

III

But from out the Main Ocean there rolled a great
    cloud,
So he clawed into Milford Haven by the Fog Blast
    so loud,

132

THE CHAUNTY OF THE " NONA "

Until he dropped anchor in a deep-wooded bay,
Where all night with Old Sleep and Quiet Sadness
    he lay—
Where all night with Old Sleep and Quiet Sadness
    he lay.

IV

Next morning was a Doldrum, and he whistled for
    a breeze,
Which came from the Nor' Nor' Westward all across
    the high seas ;
And in passing St Govan's lightship he gave them
    good night,
But before it was morning he raised Lundy Light—
Before it was morning he had raised Lundy Light.

V

Then he tossed for twelve hours in that horrible place
Which is known to the Mariner as the Great White
    Horse Race,
Till with a slant about three bells, or maybe near
    four,
He saw white water breaking upon Loud Appledore—
He saw white water breaking upon Loud Appledore.

VI

The Pirates of Appledore, the Wines of Instow ;
But her nose is for Bideford with the tide at the flow.

133

THE CHAUNTY OF THE " NONA "

Rattle anchor, batten hatches, and falls all lie
    curled.
The Long Bridge of Bideford is the end of the
    World—
The Long Bridge of Bideford is the end of the World.

THE WINGED HORSE

I

It's ten years ago to-day you turned me out o' doors
To cut my feet on flinty lands and stumble down
 the shores,
And I thought about the all-in-all, oh more than I
 can tell!
But I caught a horse to ride upon and I rode him very
 well,
He had flame behind the eyes of him and wings upon
 his side.
  And I ride, and I ride!

II

I rode him out of Wantage and I rode him up the hill,
And there I saw the Beacon in the morning standing
 still,
Inkpen and Hackpen and southward and away
High through the middle airs in the strengthening
 of the day,
And there I saw the channel-glint and England
 her pride.
  And I ride, and I ride!

135

THE WINGED HORSE

III

And once a-top of Lambourne down toward the hill
    of Clere
I saw the Host of Heaven in rank and Michael with
    his spear,
And Turpin out of Gascony and Charlemagne the
    Lord,
And Roland of the marches with his hand upon his
    sword
For the time he should have need of it, and forty
    more beside.
            And I ride, and I ride!

IV

For you that took the all-in-all the things you left
    were three.
A loud voice for singing and keen eyes to see,
And a spouting well of joy within that never yet
    was dried!
            And I ride.

STREPHON'S SONG

(FROM " THE CRUEL SHEPHERDESS "

WHEN I was not much older
Than Cupid, but bolder,
I asked of his Mother in passing her bower
What it was in their blindness
Men asked of her kindness
And she said it was nought but a delicate flower:
Such a delicate, delicate, delicate flower!

This morning you kissed me,
By noon you dismissed me
As though such great things were the jest of one hour,
And you left me still wondering
If I were not too blundering
To deal with that delicate, delicate flower:
'Tis such a delicate, delicate, delicate flower!

For if that's the complexion
Of Ladies' affection
I must needs be a fool to remain in their power;
But there's that in me burning
Which brings me returning
To beg for the delicate, delicate flower;
To implore for that delicate, delicate flower!

THE CIGADAS

MUCH louder was the Song of the Cigadas
    Upon the Mountain-side, before the day:
The Mountain-side between the two Posadas,
    The two Posadas on Puerto Bay.
    I hear the Sussex Crickets in the hay.
Much louder was the song of the Cigadas.

THE ISLANDS

Sing to me of the Islands, O daughter of Cohoolin,
    sing.
        Sing to me of the West :
Sing to me of the girth loosened and the lax harp
    string
        And of rest.

Beyond the skerries and beyond the outer water
        There lies the land.
Sing to me of the Islands, O daughter of Cohoolin, O
    High King's daughter.
        And of the Overstrand.

I desire to be with Brandan and his companions in
    the quiet places.
        And to drink of their Spring.
Sing to me of the Islands and of the Blessed Faces
        O Daughter of Cohoolin sing !

THE FIRE

I

WE rode together all in pride,
They laughing in their riding gowns
We young men laughing at their side,
We charged at will across the downs.

II

We were companions. We were young.
We were immortal—so we said. . . .
For that which in the heart was sung
Could have no commerce with the Dead.

III

Oh! We should live for ever!—Yes!
We were immortal—till there came
Command imposing loneliness
And an extinction of the flame.

IV

And now it's over . . . How it rains!
And now it's over. Though the gale
Gives as of old its gallant hail,
A-driving at the window panes.

140

THE FIRE

V

Lord! How the business disappears!
The golden faces charged with sense
Have broken to accept the years.
And look! what comes to Innocence!

VI

The chosen pictures I retain
Shall perish quickly as shall I.
Only a little while remain
The Downs in their solemnity.

VII

Were they not here, the girls and boys?
I hear them.   They are at my call.
The stairs are full of ghostly noise,
But there is no one in the hall.

VIII

The firelight sinks: a reddening shade:
I watch alone beside the fire:
The fire of my good oak is made:
Where is the flower of my desire?

THE FIRE

IX

A canker caught it at the root:
A twisted stock: a barren Briar.
It withered.   It will bear no fruit.
Where is the flower of my desire?

X

Absolve me, God, that in the land
Which I can nor regard nor know
Nor think about nor understand,
The flower of my desire shall blow.

IV
BALLADES

SHORT BALLADE AND
POSTSCRIPT ON CONSOLS AND BOERS

I

GIGANTIC daughter of the West
  (The phrase is Tennysonian), who
From this unconquerable breast
  The vigorous milk of Freedom drew
—We gave it freely—shall the crest
  Of Empire in your keeping true,
Shall England—I forget the rest,
  But Consols are at 82.

II

Now why should anyone invest,
  As even City people do
(His Lordship did among the rest),
  When stocks—but what is that to you ?
And then, who ever could have guessed
  About the guns—and horses too !—
Besides, they knew their business best,
  And Consols are at 82.

III

It serves no purpose to protest,
    It isn't manners to halloo
About the way the thing was messed—
    Or vaguely call a man a Jew.
A gentleman who cannot jest
    Remarked that we should muddle through
(The continent was much impressed),
    And Consols are at 82.

Envoi

Prince Botha lay at Pilgrim's Rest
    And Myberg in the Great Karroo
(A desert to the south and west),
    And Consols are at 82.

Postscript

Permit me—if you do not mind—
    To add it would be screaming fun
If, after printing this, I find
    Them after all at 81.

Or 70 or 63,
    Or 55 or 44,
Or 39 and going free,
    Or 28—or even more.

BALLADE AND POSTSCRIPT ON CONSOLS

Further Envoi

No matter—take no more advice
   From doubtful and intriguing men.
Refuse the stuff at any price,
   And slowly watch them fall to 10.

Meanwhile I feel a certain zest
   In writing once again the new
Refrain that all is for the best,
   And Consols are at 82.

Last Envoi

Prince, you and I were barely thirty-three,
   And now I muse and wonder if it's true,
That you were you and I myself was me,
   And 3 per cents were really 82!

BALLADE OF THE UNANSWERED QUESTION

I

WHAT dwelling hath Sir Harland Pott
  That died of drinking in Bungay ?
Nathaniel Goacher who was shot
  Towards the end of Malplaquet ?
The only thing that we can say,
  (The only thing that has been said)
About these gentlemen is " Nay ! "
  But where are the unanswering dead ?

II

Lord Bumplepuppy, too, that got
  The knock from Messrs Dawkins' dray ?
And Jonas, whom the Cachalot
  Begulphed in Esdraelon Bay ?
The Calvinistic John McKay,
  Who argued till his nostrils bled,
And dropped in apoplexy ?   Nay !
  But where are the unanswering dead ?

BALLADE OF THE UNANSWERED QUESTION

III

And Heliodorus too, that hot
   Defender of the Roman sway;
And He, the author of the " *Tot*
   Mercedes dant Victoriæ,"
And all the armoured squadrons gay
   That ever glory nourishèd
In all the world's high charges ? Nay !
   But where are the unanswering dead ?

Envoi

Prince, have you ever learnt to pray
   Upon your knees beside your bed ?
You miserable waxwork ? Nay !
   But where are the unanswering dead ?

BALLADE TO OUR LADY OF CZESTOCHOWA

I

Lady and Queen and Mystery manifold
    And very Regent of the untroubled sky,
Whom in a dream St Hilda did behold
    And heard a woodland music passing by:
    You shall receive me when the clouds are high
With evening and the sheep attain the fold.
This is the faith that I have held and hold,
    And this is that in which I mean to die.

II

Steep are the seas and savaging and cold
    In broken waters terrible to try;
And vast against the winter night the wold,
    And harbourless for any sail to lie.
    But you shall lead me to the lights, and I
Shall hymn you in a harbour story told.
This is the faith that I have held and hold,
    And this is that in which I mean to die.

BALLADE TO OUR LADY OF CZESTOCHOWA

III

Help of the half-defeated, House of gold,
    Shrine of the Sword, and Tower of Ivory;
Splendour apart, supreme and aureoled,
    The Battler's vision and the World's reply.
    You shall restore me, O my last Ally,
To vengence and the glories of the bold.
This is the faith that I have held and hold,
    And this is that in which I mean to die.

Envoi

Prince of the degradations, bought and sold,
    These verses, written in your crumbling sty,
Proclaim the faith that I have held and hold
And publish that in which I mean to die.

BALLADE OF HELL AND OF MRS ROEBECK

I

I'M going out to dine at Gray's
    With Bertie Morden, Charles and Kit,
And Manderly who never pays,
    And Jane who wins in spite of it,
    And Algernon who won't admit
The truth about his curious hair
    And teeth that very nearly fit :—
And Mrs Roebeck will be there.

II

And then to-morrow someone says
    That someone else has made a hit
In one of Mister Twister's plays.
    And off we go to yawn at it ;
    And when it's petered out we quit
For number 20, Taunton Square,
    And smoke, and drink, and dance a bit :—
And Mrs Roebeck will be there.

152

BALLADE OF HELL AND OF MRS ROEBECK

III

And so through each declining phase
  Of emptied effort, jaded wit,
And day by day of London days
  Obscurely, more obscurely, lit;
  Until the uncertain shadows flit
Announcing to the shuddering air
  A Darkening, and the end of it :—
And Mrs Roebeck will be there.

Envoi

Prince, on their iron thrones they sit,
  Impassible to our despair,
The dreadful Guardians of the Pit :—
  And Mrs Roebeck will be there.

BALLADE OF UNSUCCESSFUL MEN

I

THE cause of all the poor in '93:
  The cause of all the world at Waterloo:
The shouts of what was terrible and free
  Behind the guns of *Vengeance* and her crew:
The Maid that rode so straightly and so true
  And broke the line to pieces in her pride—
They had to chuck it up; it wouldn't do;
  The Devil didn't like them, and they died.

II

Cæsar and Alexander shall agree
  That right athwart the world their bugles blew:
And all the lads that marched in Lombardy
  Behind the young Napoleon charging through:
All that were easy swordsmen, all that slew
  The Monsters, and that served our God and tried
The temper of this world—they lost the clue.
  The Devil didn't like them, and they died.

154

BALLADE OF UNSUCCESSFUL MEN

III

You, the strong sons of anger and the sea,
 What darkness on the wings of battle flew ?
Then the great dead made answer : " Also we
 With Nelson found oblivion : Nelson, who
When cheering out of port in spirit grew
 To make one purpose with the wind and tide—
Our nameless hulks are sunk and rotted through
 The Devil didn't like us and we died."

Envoi

Prince, may I venture (since it's only you)
 To speak discreetly of The Crucified ?
He was extremely unsuccessful too :
 The Devil didn't like Him, and He died.

BALLADE OF THE HERESIARCHS

I

John Calvin whose peculiar fad
    It was to call God murderous,
Which further led that feverish cad
    To burn alive the Servetus.
The horrible Bohemian Huss,
    the Tedious Wycliffe, where are they ?
But where is old Nestorius ?
    The wind has blown them all away.

II

The Kohen out of Novdograd
    Who argued from the Roman Jus
" *Privata fasta nihil ad*
    Rem nisi sint de sacribus."
And Hume, who made a dreadful fuss
    About the Resurrection Day
And said it was ridiculous—
    The wind has blown them all away.

156

BALLADE OF THE HERESIARCHS

III

Of Smith the gallant Mormon lad
    That took of wives an over-plus:
Johanna Southcott who was mad
    And nasty Nietzsche, who was worse.
Of Tolstoy, the Eccentric Russ,
    Our strong Posterity shall say:
" Lord Jesus!   What are these to us ?
    The wind has blown them all away ! "

Envoi

Prince, should you meet upon a bus
    A man who makes a great display
Of Dr Haeckel, argue thus :—
    The wind has blown them all away.

BALLADE OF GOOD TIDINGS

The other day the £ fell out of bed
With consequences that are far from clear;
For instance, Eldorado Deeps, instead
Of jumping up, incline to lurch and veer;
And while Commander Turtle thinks it queer
Professor Guff is willing to explain;
But anyhow, the quiet profiteer
Will miss the Riviera and Champagne.

The out o'work will miss his loaf of bread,
The half-at-work will miss his glass of beer,
The City clerk—who might as well be dead—
Will miss the slight advance in his career,
And very many of my friends, I fear,
(Like Algernon, who hasn't got a brain)
A'pacing hollow-eyed on Brighton Pier,
Will miss the Riviera and Champagne.

Ladies and Lords who once on glory fed,
Renaldo, Pharamond and Guinevere,
And Francis, that in glittering armour led
The long defile of Lance and Halbadier;
High Captains of an elder world, give ear—

BALLADE OF GOOD TIDINGS

Cæsar and Bonaparte and Charlemagne—
The nobler masters of our modern sphere
Will miss the Riviera and Champagne.

Envoi

Prince, Oh my Prince, 'Tis heavenly to hear!
Stroke the piano; croon it once again   .
" The Rich, the Very Rich, this very year„
Will miss the Riviera and Champagne."

BALLADE OF ILLEGAL ORNAMENTS

" . . . the controversy was ended by His Lordship, who wrote to the Incumbent ordering him to remove from the Church all Illegal Ornaments at once, and especially a Female Figure with a Child."

I

WHEN that the Eternal deigned to look
    On us poor folk to make us free,
He chose a Maiden, whom He took
    From Nazareth in Galilee;
    Since when the Islands of the Sea,
The Field, the City, and the Wild
    Proclaim aloud triumphantly
A Female Figure with a Child.

II

These Mysteries profoundly shook
    The Reverend Doctor Leigh, D.D.,
Who therefore stuck into a Nook
    (or Niche) of his Incumbency
    An Image filled with majesty
To represent the Undefiled,
    The Universal Mother—She—
A Female Figure with a Child.

BALLADE OF ILLEGAL ORNAMENTS

III

His Bishop, having read a book
  Which proved as plain as plain could be
That all the Mutts had been mistook
  Who talked about a Trinity,
  Wrote off at once to Doctor Leigh
In manner very far from mild,
  And said: " Remove them instantly !
A Female Figure with a Child ! "

Envoi

Prince Jesus, in mine Agony,
  Permit me, broken and defiled,
Through blurred and glazing eyes to see
  A Female Figure with a Child.

V
EPIGRAMS

V

EPIGRAMS

EPIGRAMS

I

On His Books

WHEN I am dead, I hope it may be said:
" His sins were scarlet, but his books were read."

II

On Noman, a Guest

Dear Mr Noman, does it ever strike you,
The more we see of you, the less we like you?

III

A Trinity

Of three in One and One in three
My narrow mind would doubting be
Till Beauty, Grace and Kindness met
And all at once were Juliet.

IV

On Torture, a Public Singer

Torture will give a dozen pence or more
To keep a drab from bawling at his door.
The public taste is quite a different thing—
Torture is positively paid to sing.

EPIGRAMS

V

On Paunch, a Parasite

Paunch talks against good liquor to excess,
And then about his raving Patroness;
And then he talks about himself. And then
We turn the conversation on to men.

VI

On Hygiene

Of old when folk lay sick and sorely tried
The doctors gave them physic, and they died.
But here's a happier age: for now we know
Both how to make men sick and keep them so.

VII

On Lady Poltagrue, a Public Peril

The Devil, having nothing else to do,
Went off to tempt My Lady Poltagrue.
My Lady, tempted by a private whim,
To his extreme annoyance, tempted him.

VIII

The Mirror

The mirror held your fair, my Fair,
A fickle moment's space.
You looked into mine eyes, and there
For ever fixed your face.

166

EPIGRAMS

Keep rather to your looking-glass
Than my more constant eyes :
It told the truth—Alas ! my lass,
My faithful memory lies.

IX
The Elm

This is the place where Dorothea smiled.
I did not know the reason, nor did she.
But there she stood, and turned, and smiled at me :
A sudden glory had bewitched the child.
The corn at harvest, and a single tree.
This is the place where Dorothea smiled.

X
The Telephone

To-night in million-voicèd London I
Was lonely as the million-pointed sky
Until your single voice.   Ah !   So the sun
Peoples all heaven, although he be but one.

XI
The Statue

When we are dead, some Hunting-boy will pass
And find a stone half-hidden in tall grass
And grey with age : but having seen that stone
(Which was your image), ride more slowly on.

EPIGRAMS

XII

Epitaph on the Favourite Dog of a Politician

Here lies a Dog : may every Dog that dies
Lie in security—as this Dog lies.

XIII

Epitaph on the Politician Himself

Here richly, with ridiculous display,
The Politician's corpse was laid away.
While all of his acquaintance sneered and slanged
I wept : for I had longed to see him hanged.

XIV

Another on the Same

This, the last ornament among the peers,
Bribed, bullied, swindled and blackmailed for years :
But Death's what even Politicians fail
To bribe or swindle, bully or blackmail.

XV

On Mundane Acquaintances

Good morning, Algernon : Good morning, Percy.
Good morning, Mrs Roebeck. Christ have mercy !

EPIGRAMS

XVI

On a Rose for Her Bosom

Go, lovely rose, and tell the lovelier fair
That he which loved her most was never there.

XVII

On the Little God

Of all the gods that gave me all their glories
To-day there deigns to walk with me but one.
I lead him by the hand and tell him stories.
It is the Queen of Cyprus' little son.

XVIII

On a Prophet

Of old 'twas Samuel sought the Lord : to-day
The Lord runs after Samuel—so they say.

XIX

On a Dead Hostess

Of this bad world the loveliest and the best
Has smiled and said " Good Night," and gone to rest.

M   169

EPIGRAMS

XX

On a General Election

The accursèd power which stands on Privilege
(And goes with Women, and Champagne and Bridge)
Broke—and Democracy resumed her reign:
(Which goes with Bridge, and Women and
    Champagne).

XXI

On a Mistaken Mariner

He whistled thrice to pass the Morning Star,
Thinking that near which was so very far.
So I, whenas I meet my Dearest Dear,
Still think that far which is so very near.

XXII

On a Sleeping Friend

Lady, when your lovely head
Droops to sink among the Dead,
And the quiet places keep
You that so divinely sleep;
Then the dead shall blessèd be
With a new solemnity,
For such Beauty, so descending,

Pledges them that Death is ending.
Sleep your fill—but when you wake
Dawn shall over Lethe break.

XXIII

Fatigue

I'm tired of Love : I'm still more tired of Rhyme.
But Money gives me pleasure all the time.

XXIV

On Benicia, who Wished Him Well

Benicia wished me well; I wished her well.
And what I wished her more I may not tell.

XXV

The False Heart

I said to Heart, " How goes it ? "   Heart replied :
" Right as a Ribstone Pippin ! "   But it lied.

XXVI

Partly from the Greek

She would be as the stars in your sight
That turn in the endless hollow ;
That tremble, and always follow
The quiet wheels of the Night.

171

EPIGRAMS

XXVII

From the Same

Love's self is sad.   Love's lack is sadder still.
But Love unloved, O, that's the greatest ill!

XXVIII

Partly from the Latin

Suns may set and suns may rise,
Our poor eyes
When their little light is past
Droop and go to sleep at last.

XXIX

Her Final Role

This man's desire; that other's hopeless end;
A third's capricious tyrant: and my friend.

XXX

On Eyes

Dark eyes adventure bring; the blue serene
Do promise Paradise: and yours are green.

EPIGRAMS

XXXI

On a Hand

Her hand which touched my hand she moved away.
But there it lies, for ever and a day.

XXXII

Obeam Libens

Insult, despise me; what you can't prevent
Is that my verse shall be your monument.
But, Oh my torment, if you treat me true
I'll cancel every line, for love of you.

XXXIII

On the Ladies of Pixton

Three Graces; and the mother were a Grace,
But for profounder meaning in her face.

XXXIV

The Diamond

This diamond, Juliet, will adorn
Ephemeral beauties yet unborn.
While my strong verse, for ever new,
Shall still adorn immortal you.

173

EPIGRAMS

XXXV

The Fragment

Towards the evening of her splendid day
Those who are little children now shall say
(Finding this verse), " Who wrote it, Juliet ? "
And Juliet answer gently, " I forget."

XXXVI

On Vital Statistics

" *Ill* fares the land to hasting *ills* a prey [1]
Where wealth accumulates and men decay."
But how much more unfortunate are those
Where wealth declines and population grows !

XXXVII

Criterion

When you are mixed with many I descry
A single light, and judge the rest thereby.
But when you are alone with me, why then,
I quite forget all women and all men.

[1] This line is execrable ; and I note it.
I quote it as the faulty poet wrote it.

EPIGRAMS

XXXVIII
The Face

A face Sir Joshua might have painted! Yea:
Sir Joshua painted anything for pay . . .
And after all you're painted every day.

XXXIX
On a Great House

These are the lawns where Cœlia lived and moved ;
Was loved, and lovely was : but never loved.

XL
On Two Ministers of State

Lump says that Caliban's of gutter breed,
And Caliban says Lump's a fool indeed,
And Caliban, and Lump and I are all agreed.

XLI
On Chelsea

I am assured by Dauber's wife
That Dauber's always true to life.
I think his wife would far prefer
That Dauber should be true to her.

175

EPIGRAMS

XLII

The Pacifist

Pale Ebenezer thought it wrong to fight,
But Roaring Bill (who killed him) thought it right.

XLIII

On another Politician

The politician, dead and turned to clay
Will make a clout to keep the wind away.
I am not fond of draughts, and yet I doubt
If I could get myself to touch that clout.

XLIV

On yet Another

Fame to her darling Shifter glory gives;
And Shifter is immortal, while he lives.

XLV

On a Puritan

He served his God so faithfully and well
That now he sees him face to face, in hell.

EPIGRAMS

XLVI

On the little God

The love of God which leads to realms above
Is contre-carréd by the God of Love.

XLVII

On a Sundial

In soft deluding lies let fools delight.
A Shadow marks our days ; which end in Night.

XLVIII

On the Same

How slow the Shadow creeps : but when 'tis past
How fast the Shadows fall.   How fast ! How fast !

XLIX

On the Same

Loss and Possession, Death and Life are one.
There falls no shadow where there shines no sun.

L

On the Same

Stealthy the silent hours advance, and still ;
And each may wound you, and the last shall kill.

EPIGRAMS

LI

On the Same

Here in a lonely glade, forgotten, I
Mark the tremendous process of the sky.
So does your inmost soul, forgotten, mark
The Dawn, the Noon, the coming of the Dark.

LII

On the Same

I that still point to one enduring star
Abandoned am, as all the Constant are.

LIII

On the Same

Save on the rare occasions when the Sun
Is shining, I am only here for fun.

LIV

On the Same

I am a sundial, and I make a botch
Of what is done far better by a watch.

178

EPIGRAMS

LV

On the Same

I am a sundial, turned the wrong way round.
I cost my foolish mistress fifty pound.

LVI

On a Great Name

I heard to-day Godolphin say
He never gave himself away.
Come, come Godolphin, scion of kings,
Be generous in little things.

LVII

Is there any reward ?
　I'm beginning to doubt it.
I am broken and bored,
　Is there any reward ?
Reassure me, Good Lord,
　And inform me about it,
Is there any reward ?
　I'm beginning to doubt it.

LVIII

In Barbary when I was young
　A woman singing through the night,
The scented lemon trees among
　In Barbary when I was young.

179

EPIGRAMS

The song that in the night was sung,
   By Lailah the Rahabite.
In Barbary when I was young,
   A woman singing through the night.

LIX

Habitations

Kings live in Palaces, and Pigs in sties,
And youth in Expectation.   Youth is wise.

LX

From the Latin (but not so pagan)

Blessed is he that has come to the heart of the
   world and is humble.
He shall stand alone; and beneath
His feet are implacable fate, and panic at night,
   and the strumble
Of the hungry river of death.

DISCOVERY

LIFE is a long discovery, isn't it?
You only get your wisdom bit by bit.
If you have luck you find in early youth
How dangerous it is to tell the Truth;
And next you learn how dignity and peace
Are the ripe fruits of patient avarice.
You find that middle life goes racing past.
You find despair: and, at the very last,
You find as you are giving up the ghost
That those who loved you best despised you
    most.

VI
THE BALLAD OF VAL-ÈS-DUNES

THE BALLAD OF VAL-ÈS-DUNES

THE VICTORY OF WILLIAM THE CONQUEROR IN HIS
YOUTH OVER THE REBELS AT VAL-ÈS-DUNES IN
THE YEAR 1047

[This piece of verse is grossly unhistorical. Val-ès-Dunes is not on the sea but inland. No Norman blazoned a shield or a church window in the middle eleventh century, still less would he frame one in silver, and I doubt gilt spurs. It was not the young Bastard of Falaise, but the men of the King in Paris that really won the battle. There was nothing Scandinavian left in Normandy, and whatever there had been five generations before was slight. The Colentin had no more Scandinavian blood than the rest. There is no such place as Longuevaile. There is a Hauteville, but it has no bay and had nothing to do with the Harcourts, and the Harcourts were not of Blood Royal—and so forth.]

I

THE men that lived in Longuevaile
　Came out to fight by bands.
They jangled all in welded mail,
Their shields were rimmed of silver pale
And blazoned like a church-vitrail :
　Their swords were in their hands.
But the harsh raven of the Old Gods
　Was on the rank sea-sands.

.　　.　　.　　.　　.　　.

THE BALLAD OF VAL-ÈS-DUNES

There rose a wind on heath and den:
The sky went racing grey.
The Bastard and his wall of men
Were a charger's course away.

II

The Old Gods of the Northern Hall
  Are in their narrow room.
Their thrones are flanked of spearmen tall,
The three that have them in their thrall,
Sit silently before them all,
  They weave upon their loom;
And round about them as they weave
  The Scalds sing doom.

III

The Bastard out of Normandy
  Was angry for his wrong.
His eyes were virginal to see,
For nothing in his heart had he
But a hunger for his great degree;
  And his back was broad and strong
As are the oxen of the field,
  That pull the ploughs along.

IV

He saw that column of cavalry wheel,
  Split outward, and deploy.

186

He heard, he heard the Oliphant peal.
He crooked an angry knee to feel
The scabbard against his gilded heel.
   He had great joy :
And he stood upright in the stirrup steel.
   Because he was a boy.

.   .   .   .   .   .

We faced their ordering, all the force,
   And there was little sound ;
But Haribert-Le-Marshall's horse
   Pawed heavily the ground.

V

As the broad ships out of Barbary
   Come driving from the large,
With yards a-bend and courses free,
And tumbling down their decks a-lee
The hurrahing of the exultant sea.
   So drave they to the charge.
But the harsh raven of the Old Gods
   Was on the rank sea-marge.

VI

The old Gods of the Northern Hall
   Are crownéd for the tomb.
Their biers are flanked of torches tall,
And through the flames that leap and fall.

THE BALLAD OF VAL-ÈS-DUNES

There comes a droning and a call
   To the night's womb,
As the tide beneath a castle wall
   Goes drumming through the gloom.

VII

They tonsured me but Easter year,
   I swore to Christ and Rome.
My name is not mine older name . . .
But ah! to see them as they came,
With thundering and with points aflame,
   I smelt foam.
And my heart was like a wandering man's,
Who piles his boat on Moorna sands
   And serves a slave in alien lands,
And then beneath a harper's hands
   Hears suddenly of home.

  •   •   •   •   •   •

   For their cavalry came in a curling leaf,
     They shouted as they drave,
   And the Bastard's line was like a reef
     But theirs was like a wave.

VIII

As the broad ships out of Barbary
   Strike rock.
And the stem shatters, and the sail flaps;
Streaming seaward; and the taut shroud snaps,

THE BALLAD OF VAL-ÈS-DUNES

And the block
  Clatters to the deck of the wreck.
So did the men of Longuevaile
  Take the shock.

IX

Our long line quivered but it did not break,
  It countered and was strong.
The first bolt went through the wind with a wail,
And another and a-many with a thudding on the
    mail;
Pattered all the arrows in an April hail;
  Whistled the ball and thong:
And I, the priest, with that began
  The singing of my song.

X

Press inward, inward, Normandy;
  Press inward, Cleres and Vaux;
Press inward, Mons and Valery;
  Press inward, Yvetot.
Stand hard the men of the Beechen Ford
(Oh! William of Falaise, my lord!)
Battle is a net and a struggle in a cord.
  Battle is a wrestler's throw.

189

The middle holding as the wings made good,
The far wings closing as the centre stood.
Battle is a mist and battle is a wood,
    And battle is won so.

XI

The fishermen fish in the River of Seine,
    They haul the long nets in.
They haul them in and they haul again,
(The fishermen fish in the River of Seine)
They haul them in and they haul again,
    A million glittering fin :
With the hauling in of our straining ends
    That Victory did begin.

XII

The tall son of the Seven Winds
    Galloped hot-foot from the Hither Hithe.
So strongly went he down the press,
Almost he did that day redress
With his holping and his hardiness,
    For his sword was like a scythe
In Arques when the grass is high,
And all the swaithes in order lie,
And there's the bailiff standing by—
    A gathering of the tithe.

XIII

And now, go forward, Normandy,
  Go forward all in one.
The press was caught and trampled and it broke
From the sword and its swinger and the axe's stroke,
Pouring through the gap in a whirl of smoke
  As a blinded herd will run.
And so fled many and a very few
With mounts all spent would staggering pursue,
But the race fell scattered as the evening grew:
  The battle was over and done.

    .   .   .   .   .   .

Like birds against the reddening day
  They dwindled one by one,
And I heard a trumpet far away
  At the setting of the sun.

    .   .   .   .   .   .

XIV

The stars were in the Eternal Sky,
  It was calm in Massared;
Richard, Abbot of Leclair, and I
And a Picard Priest that held on high
  A Torch above his head;
We stumbled through the darkening land
Assoiling with anointed hand
  The dying and the dead.

191

THE BALLAD OF VAL-ÈS-DUNES

XV

How many in the tufted grass,
　　How many dead there lay.
For there was found the Fortenbras
And young Garain of Hault, alas !
And the Wardens of the Breton pass
　　Who were lords of his array,
And Hugh that trusted in his glass
　　But came not home the day.

XVI

I saw the miller of Martindall,
　　I saw that archer die.
The blunt quarrel caught him at the low white wall,
And he tossed up his arrow to the Lord God of all,
But long before the first could fall
　　His soul was in the sky.

XVII

The last of all the lords that sprang
　　From Harcourt of the Crown,
He parried with the shield and the silver rang,
But the axe fell heavy on the helm with a clang
And the girths parted and the saddle swang,
　　And he went down :
　　He never more sang winter songs
　　In his high town.

192

XVIII

In his high town that Faëry is,
　　And stands on Harcourt bay,
The fisher surging through the night
Takes bearing by that castle height,
And moors him harboured in the bight,
　　And watches for the day.
But with the broadening of the light,
　　It vanishes away.

XIX

In his high town that Faëry is,
　　And stands on Harcourt Lea.
To summon him up his arrier-ban,
His writ beyond the mountains ran;
My father was his serving man,
　　Although the farm was free.
Before the angry wars began
　　He was a friend to me.

XX

The night before the boy was born
　　There came a Priest who said
That he had seen red Aldeborn,
The star of hate in Taurus' horn,

THE BALLAD OF VAL-ÈS-DUNES

Which glared above a field of corn,
  And covered him with dread.
I wish to God I had not held
  The cloth in which he bled.

* * * * *

XXI

The Horse from Cleres and Valery,
  The foot from Yvetot,
And all the men of the Harbour Towns
  That live by fall and flow.
And all the men of the Beechen Ford
—Oh! William of Falaise, my lord!—
And all the sails in Michael's ward,
And all the shields of Caux,
  Shall follow you out across the world,
  With sword and lance and bow,
To Beachy and to Pevensey Bar,
  To Chester through the snow,
With sack and pack and camping tent,
  A-grumbling as they go:
My lord is William of Falaise.
  Haro!

HEROIC POEM IN PRAISE OF WINE

To Duff Cooper

To exalt, enthrone, establish and defend,
To welcome home mankind's mysterious friend:
Wine, true begetter of all arts that be;
Wine, privilege of the completely free;
Wine the recorder; wine the sagely strong;
Wine, bright avenger of sly-dealing wrong,
Awake, Ausonian Muse, and sing the vineyard song!

Sing how the Charioteer from Asia came,
And on his front the little dancing flame
Which marked the God-head. Sing the Panther-
    team,
The gilded Thyrsus twirling, and the gleam
Of cymbals through the darkness. Sing the drums.
He comes: the young renewer of Hellas comes!
The Seas await him. Those Aegean Seas
Roll from the dawning, ponderous, ill at ease,
In lifts of lead, whose cresting hardly breaks
To ghostly foam, when suddenly there awakes
A mountain glory inland. All the skies
Are luminous; and amid the sea bird cries

HEROIC POEM IN PRAISE OF WINE

The mariner hears a morning breeze arise.
Then goes the Pageant forward.   The sea-way
Silvers the feet of that august array
Trailing above the waters, through the airs;
And as they pass a wind before them bears
The quickening word, the influence magical.
The Islands have received it, marble-tall;
The long shores of the mainland.   Something fills
The warm Euboean combes, the sacred hills
Of Aulis and of Argos.   Still they move
Touching the City walls, the Temple grove,
Till, far upon the horizon-glint, a gleam
Of light, of trembling light, revealed they seem
Turned to a cloud, but to a cloud that shines,
And everywhere as they pass, the Vines !   The Vines !
The Vines, the conquering Vines ! And the Vine
    breathes
Her savour through the upland, empty heaths
Of treeless wastes; the Vines have come to where
The dark Pelasgian steep defends the lair
Of the wolf's hiding; to the empty fields
By Aufidus, the dry campaign that yields
No harvest for the husbandman, but now
Shall bear a nobler foison than the plough;
To where, festooned along the tall elm trees,
Tendrils are mirrored in Tyrrhenian seas;
To where the South awaits them; even to where
Stark, African, informed of burning air,

HEROIC POEM IN PRAISE OF WINE

Upturned to Heaven the broad Hipponian plain
Extends luxurious and invites the main.
Guelma's a mother : barren Thapsa breeds ;
And northward in the valleys, next the meads
That sleep by misty river banks, the Vines
Have struck to spread below the solemn pines.
The Vines are on the roof-trees.   All the Shrines
And Homes of men are consecrate with Vines.

And now the task of that triumphant day
Has reached to victory.   In the reddening ray
With all his train, from hard Iberian lands
Fulfilled, apparent, that Creator stands
Halted on Atlas.   Far beneath him, far,
The strength of Ocean darkening and the star
Beyond all shores.   There is a silence made.
It glorifies : and the gigantic shade
Of Hercules adores him from the West.
Dead Lucre : burnt Ambition : Wine is best.

But what are these that from the outer murk
Of dense mephitic vapours creeping lurk
To breathe foul airs from that corrupted well
Which oozes slime along the floor of Hell
These are the stricken palsied brood of sin
In whose vile veins, poor, poisonous and thin,
Decoctions of embittered hatreds crawl :
These are the Water-Drinkers, cursed all !

HEROIC POEM IN PRAISE OF WINE

On what gin-sodden Hags, what flaccid sires
Bred these White Slugs from what exhaust desires ?
In what close prison's horror were their wiles
Watched by what tyrant power with evil smiles ;
Or in what caverns, blocked from grace and air
Received they, then, the mandates of despair ?
What !   Must our race, our tragic race, that roam
All exiled from our first, and final, home :
That in one moment of temptation lost
Our heritage, and now wander, hunger-tost
Beyond the Gates (still speaking with our eyes
For ever of remembered Paradise),
Must we with every gift accepted, still,
With every joy, receive attendant ill ?
Must some lewd evil follow all our good
And muttering dog our brief beatitude ?

A primal doom, inexorable, wise,
Permitted, ordered, even these to rise.
Even in the shadow of so bright a Lord
Must swarm and propagate the filthy horde
Debased, accursed I say, abhorrent and abhorred.
Accursed and curse-bestowing.   For whosoe'er
Shall suffer their contagion, everywhere
Falls from the estate of man and finds his end
To the mere beverage of the beast condemned.
For such as these in vain the Rhine has rolled
Imperial centuries by hills of gold ;

HEROIC POEM IN PRAISE OF WINE

For such as these the flashing Rhone shall rage
In vain its lightning through the Hermitage
Or level-browed divine Touraine receive
The tribute of her vintages at eve.
For such as these Burgundian heats in vain
Swell the rich slope or load the empurpled plain.
Bootless for such as these the mighty task
Of bottling God the Father in a flask
And leading all Creation down distilled
To one small ardent sphere immensely filled.
With memories empty, with experience null,
With vapid eye-balls meaningless and dull
They pass unblest through the unfruitful light;
And when we open the bronze doors of Night,
When we in high carousal, we, reclined,
Spur up to Heaven the still ascending mind,
Pass with the all inspiring, to and fro,
The torch of genius and the Muse's glow,
They, lifeless, stare at vacancy alone
Or plan mean traffic, or repeat their moan.
We, when repose demands us, welcomed are
In young white arms, like our great Exemplar
Who, wearied with creation, takes his rest
And sinks to sleep on Ariadne's breast.
They through the darkness into darkness press
Despised, abandoned and companionless.
And when the course of either's sleep has run
We leap to life like heralds of the sun;

HEROIC POEM IN PRAISE OF WINE

We from the couch in roseate mornings gay
Salute as equals the exultant day
While they, the unworthy, unrewarded, they
The dank despisers of the Vine, arise
To watch grey dawns and mourn indifferent skies.

Forget them!   Form the Dionysian ring
And pulse the ground, and Io, Io, sing.

Father Lenæan, to whom our strength belongs,
Our loves, our wars, our laughter and our songs,
Remember our inheritance, who praise
Your glory in these last unhappy days
When beauty sickens and a muddied robe
Of baseness fouls the universal globe.
Though all the Gods indignant and their train
Abandon ruined man, do thou remain!
By thee the vesture of our life was made,
The Embattled Gate, the lordly Colonnade,
The woven fabric's gracious hues, the sound
Of trumpets, and the quivering fountain-round,
And, indestructible, the Arch, and, high,
The Shaft of Stone that stands against the sky,
And, last, the guardian-genius of them, Rhyme,
Come from beyond the world to conquer time:
All these are thine, Lenæan.

By thee do seers the inward light discern;
By thee the statue lives, the Gods return;

HEROIC POEM IN PRAISE OF WINE

By thee the thunder and the falling foam
Of loud Acquoria's torrent call to Rome;
Alba rejoices in a thousand springs,
Gensano laughs, and Orvieto sings . . .
But, Ah! With Orvieto, with that name
Of dark, Eturian, subterranean flame
The years dissolve. I am standing in that hour
Of majesty Septembral, and the power
Which swells the clusters when the nights are still
With autumn stars on Orvieto hill.

Had these been mine, Ausonian Muse, to know
The large contented oxen heaving slow;
To count my sheaves at harvest; so to spend
Perfected days in peace until the end;
With every evening's dust of gold to hear
The bells upon the pasture height, the clear
Full horn of herdsmen gathering in the kine
To ancient byres in hamlets Appenine,
And crown abundant age with generous ease:
Had these, Ausonian Muse, had these, had these . . . . .

But since I would not, since I could not stay,
Let me remember even in this my day
How, when the ephemeral vision's lure is past
All, all, must face their Passion at the last

Was there not one that did to Heaven complain
How, driving through the midnight and the rain,

HEROIC POEM IN PRAISE OF WINE

He struck, the Atlantic seethe and surge before,
Wrecked in the North along a lonely shore
To make the lights of home and hear his name no
    more.
Was there not one that from a desperate field
Rode with no guerdon but a rifted shield;
A name disherited; a broken sword;
Wounds unrenowned; battle beneath no Lord;
Strong blows, but on the void, and toil without
    reward.

When from the waste of such long labour done
I too must leave the grape-ennobling sun
And like the vineyard worker take my way
Down the long shadows of declining day,
Bend on the sombre plain my clouded sight
And leave the mountain to the advancing night,
Come to the term of all that was mine own
With nothingness before me, and alone;
Then to what hope of answer shall I turn?
Comrade-Commander whom I dared not earn,
What said You then to trembling friends and
    few?
" A moment, and I drink it with you new :
But in my Father's Kingdom."   So, my Friend,
Let not Your cup desert me in the end.
But when the hour of mine adventure's near
Just and benignant, let my youth appear